Grammar Tables

by

Peter Bendall

Published by Peter Bendall, 92 York Street, Cambridge CB1 2PY

ISBN-13: 978-0-9562127-0-2

Acknowledgements

Thanks to Diane Winkleby, Maria Dolors Romeu Font, Kathleen Hargreaves and Steve Laslett for their valuable comments and suggestions.

Contents

Outline of the English Grammar System

● Word classes

Noun	**Countable singular**	*table • bean • person • cow*
	Countable plural	*hats • children • ducks*
	Uncountable	*butter • intelligence • blood*
	Genitive	***England's*** *cities •* ***bees'*** *stings*
Pronoun	**Subject**	*I • you • he • she • it • we • they*
	Object	*me • you • him • her • it • us • them*
	Possessive	*mine • yours • his • hers • its • ours • theirs*
	Reflexive	*myself • yourself • herself • himself • ourselves • themselves*
Determiner	**Articles**	*a • an • the • Ø*
	Quantity	*five • many • few • some • hardly any*
	Possessives	*my • your • her • his • its • our • their*
	Demonstrative	*this • that • these • those*
Quantifier	**Numbers/quantities**	***a lot of*** *money •* ***masses of*** *ice-cream •* ***thousands of*** *penguins*
	Parts/pieces	***a slice of*** *cheesecake •* ***a packet of*** *crackers •* ***a bit of*** *cheese*
Adjective	**Before noun**	***big*** *feet • a* ***fantastic*** *film*
	After verb	*She is* ***naïve*** *• They seem* ***happy***
	Comparative	*tall**er** • larg**er** • happi**er***
	Superlative	*nic**est** • deep**est** • earli**est***
Preposition	**Position**	*in • under • near • above*
	Direction	*towards • away from • in the direction of*
	Movement	*through • into • out of*
	Time	*at • on • in • during • after • before*
Verb	**Auxiliary**	*do • be • have*
	Modal	*can • will • must • may • might • could • should • would*
	Stative	*be • seem • like • know • look • have*
	Dynamic	*play • go • put • drop • phone • interrogate*
Adverb	**Manner**	*slowly • carefully • fast • stupidly*
	Place	*here • there • nearby • everywhere*
	Time	*yesterday • now • sometimes*
	Degree	***really*** *nice •* ***extremely*** *silly*
Conjunction	**Co-ordinating**	*and • but • or • yet*
	Subordinating	*when • while • although • if • until • before • that*

● Phrase types (phrase heads in **bold**)

Noun phrase		*the* ***cat*** *• her* ***intelligence*** *• much of* ***England*** *• a lot of* ***water*** *• the* ***cat*** *with pointed ears* *the* ***cheese*** *which you ate • the* ***dog*** *sitting under the table • a* ***book*** *written by Fishlock* *my filthy old* ***carpet*** *•* ***Cambridge*** *United*
Prepositional phrase		***in*** *town •* ***before*** *the news •* ***up*** *the hill •* ***in*** *the dim and distant past* ***towards*** *the cat with pointed ears •* ***after*** *the party •* ***apart from*** *the grandchildren*
Adjective phrase		*highly* ***contagious*** *• relatively* ***stable*** *• less* ***expensive*** *• much* ***better*** *•* ***red*** *all over* *reddish-**brown** •* ***fed up*** *with waiting •* ***nice*** *to eat •* ***sorry*** *to say*
Verb phrase	**Non-finite**	*to* ***play*** *• to have* ***played*** *• to have been* ***playing*** *•* ***playing*** *•* ***played*** *• to be* ***playing*** *having* ***played*** *• having been* ***playing***
	Finite	***play*** *•* ***play****s • am/is/are* ***playing*** *• have/has* ***played*** *• has been* ***playing*** *•* ***played*** *was/were* ***playing*** *• had* ***played*** *• had been* ***playing*** *• will* ***play*** *• will be* ***playing*** *will have* ***played*** *• will have been* ***playing***
Adverb phrase		*really* ***nastily*** *• extremely* ***frankly*** *•* ***somewhere*** *in South America •* ***nowhere*** *to sleep*

Outline of the English Grammar System (continued)

● Clause elements

Subject (= noun phrase/ nominal clause/ non-finite clause)	*The cat* was playing *Some money* has been stolen *He* hit me *Whoever put the cake in the breadbin* is a complete idiot *Going to the dentist* is my favourite activity
Verb (= verb/verb phrase)	They***'ve gone*** to London • I ***didn't know*** what to do He definitely ***wouldn't have missed*** it You***'ll be arrested*** We ***don't seem to have*** any mustard
Object (= noun phrase/ nominal clause)	I'm going to read ***a book*** I've bought ***some cheese*** He hit ***me*** • I gave ***Fred the book*** The magistrates decided ***that he should not go to prison***
Complement (= noun/adj phrase)	About subject: <u>She</u> is ***a great tennis player*** • <u>They</u> seem ***tired*** About object: We consider <u>it</u> ***a great success*** • Don't make <u>me</u> ***angry***
Adverb (= adverb/prep phrase)	***Frankly***, I think he's lying • He reads ***really quickly*** • I'll see you ***next week*** Let's go ***home*** • She ran ***up the stairs*** • ***Financially***, we're in a mess We have decided to extend the lease ***for as long as you need it***

● Clause types 1: Independent clauses
(One independent clause = **simple sentence**; linked independent clauses = **compound sentence**)

Simple sentence	*He got up. He turned the radio off.* *I like cheesecake. I hate Chelsea buns.* *You can sleep in the spare room. You can use the sofa.*
Compound sentences	*He got up and turned the radio off* *I like cheesecake but I hate Chelsea buns* *You can sleep in the spare room or you can use the sofa*

● Clause types 2: Subordinate clauses
(Main/independent clause + Subordinate clause = **complex sentence**)

Adverbial clause	Can you call me ***when you're ready***? I'll be here by 6.00 ***unless anything happens*** We had the picnic ***although it was raining***
Relative clause	The person ***who painted my house*** lives in Leeds **(Restrictive)** These gloves, ***which I bought in a sale***, are quite warm **(Non-restrictive)**
Non-finite clause	***While waiting for the train***, I dropped my briefcase I don't know ***whether to go*** I saw him ***running down the street*** Do you really intend ***to eat that pie***?
Nominal clause	***That you failed the exam*** is not your fault ***What we want*** is more money She told me ***where I could find the orange juice*** I don't know ***who she is***

© Peter Bendall 2010

Inflections

● Nouns

Singular to plural (regular)	*dog* → **dogs** • *table* → **tables**
Singular to plural (irregular)	*foot* → **feet** • *dormouse* → **dormice**
Singular to genitive	*cat* → **cat's** • *John* → **John's**
Plural to genitive (regular)	*horses* → **horses'** • *daffodils* → **daffodils'**
Plural to genitive (irregular)	*children* → **children's** • *oxen* → **oxen's**

● Pronouns

Subject to object	*I* → **me** • *he* → **him** • *she* → **her** • *we* → **us** • *they* → **them**
Subject to possessive	*I* → **mine** • *you* → **yours** • *he* → **his** • *she* → **hers** • *we* → **ours** • *they* → **theirs**
Relative: subject to object	*who* → **whom**
Relative: subject to possessive	*who* → **whose**
Number: singular to plural	*one* → **ones**

● Determiners

Indefinite article: before vowel	*a* → **an**
Demonstrative: singular to plural	*this* → **these** • *that* → **those**
Number: cardinal to ordinal	*one* → **first** • *two* → **second** • *three* → **third** • *four* → **fourth**
Quantity: comparative	*much/many* → **more** • *few* → **fewer** • *little* → **less**

● Adjectives

Comparative (regular)	*tall* → **taller** • *big* → **bigger** • *daft* → **dafter**
Comparative (irregular)	*good* → **better** • *bad* → **worse** • *far* → **farther/further**
Superlative (regular)	*high* → **highest** • *hot* → **hottest**
Superlative (irregular)	*good* → **best** • *bad* → **worst** • *far* → **furthest**

● Full verbs

Base form to third person /z/	*play* → **plays** • *sing* → **sings** • *slide* → **slides**
Base form to third person /s/	*make* → **makes** • *sit* → **sits** • *clip* → **clips**
Base form to third person /ɪz/	*sneeze* → **sneezes** • *wish* → **wishes**
Base form to past (regular) /t/	*walk* → **walked** • *wrap* → **wrapped**
Base form to past (regular) /d/	*groan* → **groaned** • *seem* → **seemed**
Base form to past (regular) /ɪd/	*start* → **started** • *end* → **ended** • *flit* → **flitted**
Base form to past (irregular)	*eat* → **ate** • *come* → **came** • *see* → **saw**
Base form to -*ing*	*go* → **going** • *show* → **showing** • *run* → **running**
Base form to past participle (reg)	*play* → **played** • *ask* → **asked** • *decide* → **decided**
Base form to past participle (irreg)	*go* → **gone** • *write* → **written** • *make* → **made**

● Primary Auxiliary verbs

be (present)	*I* **am** • *you* **are** • *we* **are** • *they* **are** • *it* **is** • *he* **is** • *she* **is**
be (past)	*I* **was** • *he* **was** • *she* **was** • *it* **was** • *you* **were** • *we* **were** • *they* **were**
have (present)	*she* **has** • *he* **has** • *it* **has**
have (past)	**had**
do (present)	*he* **does** • *she* **does** • *it* **does**
do (past)	**did**

● Modal verbs

'Base form' to 'past'	*will* → **would** • *shall* → **should** • *can* → **could** • *may* → **might**
'Base form' to negative (contraction)	*will* → **won't** • *shall* → **shan't** • *can* → **can't** • *must* → **mustn't**
'Past' to negative (contraction)	*would* → **wouldn't** • *should* → **shouldn't** • *could* → **couldn't**

● Adverbs

Position to movement	*here* → **hence** • *there* → **thence** • *where* → **whence**
Comparative	*fast* → **faster** • *quickly* → **quicker** • *well* → **better**
Superlative	*soon* → **soonest** • *early* → **earliest** • *bad* → **worst**

Nouns: Common categories

● Countables: nouns with both singular and plural forms

Containers	*bowl • box • bag • test-tube • suitcase • vessel • cup • trunk*
Contents of space	*sun • moon • galaxy • planet • star • black hole • comet*
Groups	*bunch • crowd • litter • pack • gang • crew • shoal • pride*
Hierarchies	*order • genus • family • archbishop • bishop • priest • clause • phrase • word*
Inexact quantities	*pinch • drop • bite • touch • bit • smidgen • lump*
Living things	*lion • armadillo • freesia • amoeba • stag beetle • cauliflower*
Machines and tools	*fan • lawnmower • fork • atomiser • juicer • electric toothbrush*
Measures	*metre • pound • micron • chain • bushel • inch • kilo • joule*
Objects	*pen • vase • organ • soap-dish • hatpin • doorstop • ironing-board*
Pairs of things (plural)	*scissors • shears • glasses • earphones • trousers*
Particles	*atom • molecule • electron • grain • gene • Higgs boson*
Parts of objects	*handle • knob • index • flywheel • cover • lid • hasp • leg*
Parts of the body	*fingernail • instep • abdomen • earlobe • cuticle • pancreas*
Shapes	*triangle • square • rectangle • trapezium • oblong • oval*
Holes	*wormhole • borehole • nostril • manhole • earhole*
Types of people (objective)	*farmer • conversationalist • thinker • artist • clown • sister*
Types of people (subjective)	*idiot • madman • clown • crook • waverer • nit • fool*

● Uncountables: nouns mostly used in the singular, without indefinite article or number

Abstractions	*power • society • thought • beauty • futility • intensity*
Activities	*skating • wood-turning • scrubbing • meditation • upholstery*
Aggregates	*hair • paper • grass • spaghetti*
Appearance	*beauty • elegance • ugliness • ungainliness • smoothness*
Areas of study	*hermeneutics • medicine • chemistry • semiotics • geography*
Bodily fluids	*blood • sweat • urine • snot • vomit • milk •*
Bodily processes	*sleep • digestion • respiration • excretion • circulation*
Bodily structures	*bone • skin • tissue • muscle • collagen • cartilage*
Crime	*murder • robbery • larceny • assault • rape • fraud*
Disabilities	*illiteracy • innumeracy • amnesia • aphasia • dyslexia*
Diseases and ailments	*tuberculosis • plague • influenza • nettle-rash • scarlet fever*
Food and drink	*meat • cheese • butter • jam • wine • whisky • schnapps*
Groups of objects	*furniture • equipment • gear*
Languages	*Chinese • Basque • French • Swahili • Hindi • Estonian*
Materials and substances	*wood • tungsten • milk • gay-lussite • oxygen • sodium • plastic*
Movements	*Romanticism • Rationalism • Protestantism • Communism*
Personal characteristics	*shyness • irritability • forgetfulness • idiocy • patience*
Phases	*infancy • childhood • adolescence • adulthood • maturity • old age*
Plant mass	*seaweed • moss • ivy • plankton • mould*
Properties	*stickiness • transparency • flexibility • ductility • fluidity*
States	*anger • illness • calm • hysteria • panic • pain • misery • wealth*
Stressful events	*birth • graduation • marriage • divorce • retirement • death*
The arts	*music • literature • sculpture • ballet • photography*
Waste matter	*rubbish • garbage • trash • waste • effluent • detritus*
Weather	*rain • sunshine • sleet • hail • snow • fog • mist • smog*

● Nouns generally used with definite article (*the*)

Collective entities	*the public • the staff • the government • the bureaucracy • the mafia*
Environmental components	*the sky • the sea • the atmosphere • the biosphere*
Generic	*the elephant • the marsh fritillary • the orchid • the wheel • the bore*
Groups of people	*the elderly • the unemployed • the young • the rich • the stupid*
Means of communication	*the phone • the internet • the post • the press*

Nouns: Plural forms

Regular plurals: + -s	*table/tables • head/heads • bottle/bottles • sausage/sausages*
***ch, sh, s, x* + -es**	*branch/branches • church/churches • wish/wishes • ash/ashes* *loss/losses • bass/basses • box/boxes • tax/taxes*
***o* + -es**	*potato/potatoes • tomato/tomatoes • hero/heroes* *volcano/volcanoes • echo/echoes*
***o* + -s**	*piano/pianos • solo/solos • curio/curios • torso/torsos*
Consonant + *y* → -ies	*body/bodies • copy/copies • pasty/pasties • lady/ladies* *party/parties • poppy/poppies • folly/follies*
vowel + *y* → -s	*boy/boys • guy/guys • bay/bays • pulley/pulleys • way/ways* *joy/joys • monkey/monkeys • ray/rays • survey/surveys*
***f* → -ves**	*calf/calves • shelf/shelves • leaf/leaves • knife/knives* *thief/thieves • half/halves • sheaf/sheaves*
***f* → -fs**	*chief/chiefs • roof/roofs • proof/proofs • belief/beliefs • safe/safes*
Plural same as singular	*fish/fish • deer/deer • sheep/sheep • swine/swine* *trout/trout • salmon/salmon • cod/cod*
Change of vowel	*woman/women • man/men • mouse/mice • louse/lice* *goose/geese • foot/feet • tooth/teeth*
Addition of irregular ending	*child/children • ox/oxen*
Archaic plurals	*cow/kine • egg/eyren • eye/eyen • shoe/shoon* *house/housen •brother/brethren*
Countable -s plurals with no corresponding singular	*winnings • takings • binoculars • outskirts • trousers* *surroundings • glasses • shears • shorts*
Non-s plural with no corresponding singular	*people • police • cattle • rabble*
-s plural form, singular uncountable entity	*rabies • politics • physics • news • means • series* *aesthetics • economics • pragmatics • semiotics*
Latin/Greek plural forms	*index/indices • larva/larvae • stigma/stigmata* *phenomenon/phenomena • radius/radii*
Centuries and decades	*the 1600s • the 1890s • the thirties*
Compounds: plural first element	*passer-by/passers-by • hanger-on/hangers-on* *brother-in-law/brothers-in-law*
-s plurals of nouns ending in /p/,/t/,/k/,/f/,/θ/ = /s/ pronunciation	*lips • maps • cats • pits • sacks • hammocks • chiefs* *cliffs • maths • megaliths*
-s plurals of nouns ending in /b/,/d/,/g/,/v/,/ð/,/m/,/n/, /ŋ/, /l/ or vowel sound = /z/ pronunciation	*tabs • hands • legs • waves • teams • collisions • wings • halls* *parties • jaws • ears • swathes • deans • tongs*
-es plurals of nouns ending in /s/,/ʃ/,/tʃ/,/dʒ/ = /ɪz/ pronunciation	*glasses • rushes • branches • judges • batches • riches*

Compound Nouns

Adjective + adverb	*whiteout • blackout*
Adjective + converted verb	*remote control • hard drive • high jump • soft sell*
Adjective + noun	*greenhouse • hotplate • software • superman*
Adverb + adverb	*roundabout • whereabouts • hereafter • outback • back-up*
Adverb + noun	*in-crowd • off-roader • through trade • overhead*
Adverb + verb	*outbreak • upset • downpour • overkill • underspend*
Determiner + noun + -*er*	*no-hoper • two-header • each-wayer*
Verb + -*ing* + noun	*washing-machine • tuning fork • carving knife • sitting-room*
Minimal pair compounds	*clip-clop • pitter-patter • zig-zag • ping-pong • hip-hop*
Noun + adjective	*heir apparent • court-martial • Governor General*
Noun + adverb	*hoe-down • sun-up • sundown • cockup • leg-up*
Noun + verb + -*ing*	*binge drinking • bungee-jumping • bareback riding • speed-dating*
Noun + noun	*backpack • bus-station • dustjacket • minefield • wineglass*
Noun + verb	*nosedive • birth control • household • bus-stop*
Noun + verb + -*er*	*carpet-beater • screwdriver • potato-masher • hair-drier*
Phrase compounds	*son-in-law • so-and-so • down-and-out • marshal-at-arms*
Verb (Intransitive) + adverb	*sleep-over • sit-up • lie-in • standby • lookout • run-in*
Verb (Transitive) + adverb	*kickback • pullover • fry-up • take-away*
Verb + -*al*	*withdrawal • upheaval • rehearsal • reversal*
Verb + -*er* + adverb	*passer-by • looker-on • sitter-in • snapper-up*
Verb + verb + -*ing*	*drink-driving • kick-boxing • breakdancing*
Verb + negative	*have-nots • do-nothing • dreadnought*
Verb + noun	*pickpocket • scratchpad • hitman • keepsake • thinktank*
Verb + verb	*make-believe • fly-drive • has-been • can-do*

Determiners

Type	Scope	Singular countable noun (S)	Plural countable noun (P)	Uncountable noun (U)
Indefinite article *a, an* (S)	General reference	*a horn* *an umbrella* *a capybara*		
Definite article *the*	Particular reference	*the orange* *the kangaroo* *the knife*	*the books* *the houses* *the tiles*	*the cheese* *the wine* *the wax*
Zero article Ø (P, U)	General reference		*dogs* *tables* *owls*	*intelligence* *soup* *comfort*
Demonstratives *this, that* (S, U) *these, those* (P)	Particular reference	*this rabbit* *that sock*	*these chairs* *those carpets*	*this water* *that butter*
Possessives *my, your, his, her, its, our, their*	Particular reference	*my car* *your hat* *his nose*	*her feet* *our pets their bedrooms*	*its transparency* *her cunning* *their soap*
Interrogatives *which, whose what*	Particular reference	*Which knife?* *Whose chair?*	*What batteries?* *Which letters?*	*Whose soap?* *Which juice?*
Relative *whose*	Particular reference	*The man whose brother I know*	*The zoo whose lions died*	*The woman whose fame has spread*
Quantifying *few, many, several* (P) *little, much* (U) *some* (P, U)	Inexact quantity		*few beans* *many errors* *several soldiers* *some cats*	*little news* *(not) much plastic* *some earth*
Numbers *no* (S, P, U) *one* (S) *2+* (P)	Exact quantity	*one dog* *a single fly* *no elephant*	*five eggs* *72 sailors* *no plates*	*no meat* *no air* *zero butter*
any	Indefinite reference	*any child under 16* *any pensioner*	*any doctors* *any beans*	*any food* *any paper*
Distributive *each, every* (S) *either, neither, both* (P=2) *all* (P=3+)	Distribution	*each chicken* *neither official* *every tortoise*	*both socks* *all children*	*all music* *all oil*
Comparative *more* (P, U) *fewer* (P) *less* (U)	Comparison		*more people* *fewer beans*	*more money* *less work*

Definite and Zero Articles: Names

Definite Article

Zero Article

Definite Article		Zero Article	
The heavenly hierarchy	*The Earth, The Solar System, The Milky Way*	Galaxies and Constellations	*Andromeda, Pegasus Orion, Draco*
Basic heavenly features	*The sun, The moon The stars, The sky*	Planets and comets	*Mars, Venus, Kohoutek Halley's Comet*
Mountain ranges	*The Himalayas The Alps*	Mountains	*Everest, Mont Blanc Ben Nevis*
Deserts	*The Sahara The Taklamakan*	Moors and heaths	*Ilkley Moor Egdon Heath*
Rivers	*The Thames The Nile*	Waterfalls	*Niagara Falls Victoria Falls*
Seas	*The Mediterranean The North Sea*	Ponds and meres	*Histon Pond Soham Mere*
Oceans	*The Pacific The Indian Ocean*	Lakes	*Lake Titicaca Lake Superior*
Straits	*The Molucca Straits The Magellan Straits*	Marshes and fens	*Hackney Marshes Grunty Fen*
Gulfs and firths	*The Gulf of Mexico The Firth of Forth*	Coves and bays	*Smuggler's Cove Whitby Bay*
Currents	*The Humboldt Current The Gulf Stream*	Conduits and ditches	*Hobson's Conduit Blake's Ditch*
Canals	*The Panama Canal The Grand Union*	Lodes	*Reach Lode Quy Lode*
Ships	*The Mary Rose The Exxon Valdez*	Spaceships	*Apollo 9 Voyager 2*
Geographical Abstractions	*The North Pole The Equator*	Continents	*Asia, Africa, Europe, Antarctica*
Kingdoms, Republics	*The United Kingdom The USA, The UAE*	Names of countries	*India, China, Sweden, Holland, Senegal*
Nationalities	*The Indians The Japanese*	Languages	*Swahili, French, Basque, Urdu*
Isles and archipelagoes	*The Isle of Skye The Faroe Islands*	Single islands	*Canvey Island Staten Island*
Districts	*The Latin Quarter The Red Light District*	Towns and cities	*Durham, Halifax, Conakry, Delhi*
Major arteries	*The M40, The A15, The Old Kent Road*	Streets and roads	*Oxford Street London Road*
Towers	*The Rotunda The Eiffel Tower*	Squares/parks/circuses	*Hyde Park, Berkeley Square, Oxford Circus*
Pubs	*The Hare and Hounds The Red Lion*	Cafes and restaurants	*Brown's, Midsummer House*
Hotels	*The Dorchester The Ritz*	Palaces	*Buckingham Palace St. James's Palace*
Auditoria	*The Warner Cinema The Adelphi Theatre*	Discos and dance halls	*Fifth Avenue Taboo*
State offices	*The Queen The Prime Minister*	Ceremonial offices	*Black Rod White Feather*
Institutions	*The Church The BBC*	Universities/colleges	*Exeter University Birkbeck College*
Public services	*The Fire Service The Police, The Army*	Shops and supermarkets	*Harrod's Sainsbury's*
Public buildings	*The Guildhall The Crown Court*	Castles and stately homes	*Warwick Castle Wimpole Hall*
Religious books	*The Bible, The Koran The Bhagavad Gita*	Reference Books	*Roget's Thesaurus Brewer's Dictionary*
Newspapers	*The Guardian The Evening News*	Magazines	*Private Eye History Today*

Definite Article: other uses

Back reference	*Yesterday afternoon I saw an eagle hunting a rabbit.* **The eagle** *was very persistent, and* **the rabbit** *had no chance*
Entertainment/media (except T.V.)	*What's on at* **the cinema**? • *There's an article on spiders in* **the newspaper** *I heard it on* **the radio** • *She always wears her best dress to* **the theatre**
Features of immediate surroundings	**The plane trees** *are lovely, aren't they, darling?* **The sand** *is absolutely perfect* • **The litter** *is a disgrace*
Industry/business/trade	*He works in* **the motor trade** • **The paper industry** *is in trouble She wants to go into* **the confectionery business**
Items on a menu	*I'll have* **the pea soup***, please* • *What do you think* **the venison***'s like?* **The spotted dick** *sounds interesting* • **The roast duck***'s off, I'm afraid*
Job grades	*Could I speak to* **the manager***, please?* • *Go over to* **the clerk** *at counter 2* **The superintendent** *would like to have a word with you, sir*
Musical instruments	*She plays* **the basset horn** • *He's pretty good on* **the guitar** **The violin** *is one of the most versatile instruments*
Nouns before a defining relative clause	**The man** *I was talking to is a well-known botanist Marie Curie is* **the person** *who discovered radium*
Objects/fixtures belonging to a room or house	*I've just cleaned* **the carpet** • **The lightshade** *is a bit dirty Who's that up on* **the roof**? • **The windowsill** *is cracked*
Over/during/in + *the next/the last*	*During* **the last three years***, we have made an average profit of £1m I'll finish it in* **the next two days** • *I've had ten calls in* **the last five minutes**
Parts of a town/regions of a country	*They live in* **the suburbs** • *I'm going into* **the centre** *this afternoon They have moved to* **the North** • **The East** *is the flattest part*
Parts of machines	*Can you check* **the gears**? • **The second hand** *isn't working* **The element** *has blown* • *One of* **the blades** *is displaced*
Past/present/future	*What do you think* **the future** *holds?* • *He's just not living in* **the present** *In* **the past** *people used the phone far less often*
Permanent features of a town	*I saw him in* **the park** *with his children* • **The streets** *are full of potholes When you get to* **the bank***, turn left* • **The new library** *is opening soon*
Plants and animals (generic)	**The dandelion** *is native to Britain* • **The water vole** *is dying out* **The date palm** *doesn't grow in Europe* • **The sloth** *knows the secret of life*
Preposition + part of the body	*He hit me on* **the head** • *He's a pain in* **the neck** *Stop digging me in* **the ribs** • *She wouldn't look me in* **the eye**
Services/departments	*Did you call* **the police**? • **The fire service** *has attained 93% of its targets Hallo, this is* **the cleansing department** • **The Treasury** *has announced…*
Shops (+ 's) (Super)markets (+ Ø)	*I went to* **the butcher's** *to buy some tripe* • *She's just gone to* **the florist's** *We get all our food at* **the supermarket** • *I got these lemons from* **the market**
Start of narrative: details/identification to follow, or understood	**The street lights** *had just gone out as* **the bearded man** *climbed over* **the fence***. In* **the night sky the stars** *twinkled and in* **the distance the dogs** *barked for their supper. In* **the pub the locals** *talked about* **the moths**
Substitution	*We went to Chichester last week.* **The town** *has a charming centre We went to the Hirst exhibition last week.* **The artist** *was there in person*
Superlative	*These are* **the best dumplings** *I have ever tasted* • *He's* **the greatest** *She is* **the most accomplished musician** *in the class*
With adjectives denoting groups of people	**The rich** *are happy with their wealth* • **The old** *are rarely treated with respect* **The dispossessed** *have no chance in modern society*
With adjectives or nouns after names of monarchs	*Alexander* **the Great** • *Erik* **the Evergood** • *Heinrich* **the Illustrious** *Louis* **the Spider** • *Håkon* **the Broadshouldered** • *Chosroes* **the Short**
With noun + place adverbial	*I went to the baker's on* **the way home** • **The flight there** *was quite bumpy* **The bread here** *is full of holes* • *I'm on* **the road to Solihull**
With noun *of* noun	*Has anyone tried to measure* **the intelligence of monkeys**? **The death of the novel** *occurred about 80 years ago*
With peoples and civilisations	**The Ancient Greeks** *knew all about fate* • **The English** *eat a lot of pies* **The Danes** *are a peace-loving people* • **The Arabs** *invented zero*
With *same*	*No two spoons are exactly* **the same** • *We laughed at* **the same time** *They have* **the same style** *of running* • *We're all in* **the same boat**

Uses of the Indefinite Article and Zero Article

● Indefinite article: *a/an*

Asking for or offering a single thing	*Could I have **a fork**, please? • Would you like **a strawberry tart**?* ***A pint** of bitter and **a lemonade**, please*
Description of physical features/clothes (singular)	*He has **a long nose**, **a cleft chin** and **a high forehead*** *She was wearing **a red dress**, **a brown jacket** and **a green hat***
Exclamations with *What* + singular countable noun	*What **a nice surprise**! • What **a damned nuisance**!* *What **a fascinating experience**! • What **a fool**!*
First mention in narrative or report	***A tree** fell across the road last night* ***A man** was arrested for swearing yesterday*
Lists of singular unidentified things	*We need **a hammer**, **a screwdriver** and **a soldering iron*** *There was **a cat**, **a rabbit** and **a hamster** all in the same room*
Measures (after their cost)	*The chintz is £3.50 **a yard** • Goose eggs are £5.00 **a dozen*** *Wensleydale is £5.85 **a kilo** • Petrol is £1.18 **a litre***
Physical symptoms	*I've got **a really bad cough** • That kid's got **a runny nose*** *I'm staying in bed – I've got **a really bad headache***
Positive or negative nouns describing character/ability	*She's **a scientific genius** • The goalkeeper's **a clown*** *That man you got the green pills from is **a charlatan***
Quantifiers and partitives	***A slice** of bread would be nice • That's **a load** of rubbish* *Could I have **a scoop** of vanilla ice-cream?*
Stating someone's occupation	*He's **a teacher** • She used to be **a police officer*** *I want to be **a fridge inspector** when I grow up*
Talking about the existence of something	*There's **a lamp** in the room • York has **a famous cathedral*** *There used to be **a good bike shop** in this street*

● Indefinite article: *an*

Before *a, e, i, o, u*	***an ant** • **an effort** • **an itch** • **an orphan** • **an usher***
Before silent *h*	***an hour** • **an honour** • **an honest mistake***
Exceptions: semi-vowels	***a European** • **a one-way street** • **a union** • **a university***

● Zero article/Zero determiner

Exclamations with *What* + uncountable or plural noun	*What **nice earrings**! • What **frightful weather** we're having, Maud* *What **passion** she has when she sings! • What **delicious toast**!*
Feelings	*I feel nothing but **contempt** for him • He smashed the plate in **anger*** *It is with **great regret** that I offer my resignation*
General means of transport	*I managed to get here on **foot** • He goes everywhere by **car*** *It would be faster to go by **train** • Going by **bike** is more convenient*
General statements about abstractions	***Intelligence** can't be measured • What is **honour**? A word* ***Familiarity** breeds **contempt** • **Life** can be hard sometimes, Percy*
General statements about plural things	***Spiders** eat **flies** • **Pimples** come in various colours* ***Aardvarks** live in South Africa • **Liquorice drinks** are disgusting*
General statements about substances	*I hate **cauliflower cheese** • **Bottled water** is a complete rip-off* ***Vitamin B13** is good for you in small quantities*
Idiomatic or metaphorical use of countable nouns	*The title is at **stake** • I was out of **pocket** after that round of drinks* *These oven gloves were made by **hand** • She came in **disguise***
Institutions: function understood	*Where do you go to **school**? • He told me to go to **hell*** *She's in **hospital** at the moment • He's out of **prison** now*
Newspaper headlines: all nouns	***Baby** eats **nappy** • **Squirrels** attack **old people's home*** ***Millionaire** falls off **yacht** • **Council** apologises for **error***
Sports and games	*Do you play **croquet**, Kevin? • **Billiards** is better than **snooker*** ***Rugby** is a game for intellectuals • We can't play **bowls** here*

Quantifiers and Partitives

● Quantifiers

Comparative quantities	*more of* his awful drawings • *less of* your sauce • *fewer of* these eggs *a larger amount of* fertilizer • *a thinner slice of* Stinking Bishop
Distribution	*both of* the centipedes • *neither of* the druids • *each of* the rooms *every single one of* the broad beans
Exact quantities	*three of* your meat pies • *half of* our income • *10 per cent of* small children *six kilos of* flour • *13.46 milligrams of* sodium
Indefinite quantities	*some of* my tulips • *a number of* police officers • *a quantity of* cheese *a certain amount of* petrol • *a fair bit of* jostling
Large quantities	*many of* the dinosaurs • *a lot of* his books • *much of* my furniture *a great deal of* nonsense • *a vast amount of* paper
Majority	*most of* her possessions • *the majority of* bachelors *nearly all of* the cordial • *the best part of* two hours
Nullity	*none of* the plumbers • *not one of* the students • *not a bit of* it *no trace of* her presence • *not a drop of* water
Remainder	*the rest of* the news • *the remainder of* the stock *the residue of* his estate • *the last bit of* the newspaper
Small quantities	*little of* the paper • *few of* her possessions • *a small amount of* nutmeg *hardly any of* the cheese • *a bit of* cash
Totality	*the whole of* Australia • *all of* our umbrellas • *the whole lot of* them *the totality of* the goose population • *every last one of* the chocolates

● Partitives

Colloquial	*pots of* money • *loads of* time • *a hatful of* chances *a shedload of* money • *a fat lot of* use
Containers	*a bowl of* lentil soup • *a jug of* juice • *a crate of* bubbly *a cup of* mead • *a packet of* crackers • *a sack of* potatoes
Group	*a flock of* sheep • *a troupe of* actors • *a gang of* labourers *a herd of* buffalo • *a bunch of* fools • *a clump of* daffodils
Large piece	*a chunk of* ice • *a lump of* sticky fudge • *a ball of* rice *a slab of* meat • *this bank and shoal of* time
Line	*a row of* seats • *a queue of* customers • *a line of* poplars *a ribbon of* water • *a file of* soldiers
Literal or metaphorical liquid flow	*a jet of* water • *a torrent of* abuse • *a dribble of* custard *a trickle of* applications • *a spurt of* hot coffee • *a flood of* complaints
Mass	*a heap of* old clothes • *a sea of* troubles • *a pile of* magazines *a crowd of* pensioners • *an armful of* loot • *a shoal of* fish
Meat part	*a leg of* lamb • *a joint of* beef • *(a) shoulder of* pork • *(a) shin of* beef *(a) shank of* mutton • *a haunch of* venison
Metaphor + abstract noun	*a modicum of* sympathy • *a sliver of* hope • *tons of* determination *an ounce of* intelligence • *a crumb of* comfort • *a scrap of* decency
Portion	*part of* their income • *a bit of* wood • *a portion of* broccoli *a square of* chocolate • *a slice of* crusty cob • *a shaving of* nutmeg
Small piece or bit	*a pinch of* snuff • *a dash of* cream • *a drop of* whisky *a speck of* dust • *a scrap of* material • *a crust of* bread
Surface covering	*a lick of* paint • *a coating of* breadcrumbs • *a dusting of* snow *a covering of* tar • *a layer of* icing • *a blanket of* mist
Units of measurement	*a metre of* silk • *ten pounds of* blackberries • *six miles of* hedgerows *a ream of* paper • *a gallon of* cider • *three inches of* ice
Vegetable part or piece	*a stick of* celery • *a head of* cabbage • *an ear of* corn • *a sprig of* parsley *a grain of* rice • *a blade of* grass • *a clove of* garlic

Pronouns

● **Subject pronouns:** *I, you, he, she, it, we, they*

Before verb: statements	*I play tennis •* **She** *was born in London*
Between verbs: questions	*Did* **you** *like it? • Where do* **they** *go jogging?*

● **Object pronouns:** *me, you, him, her, it, us, them*

After verb	*The lorry hit* **him** *• We didn't tell* **her**
After verb then after *to*	*I gave it to* **them** *• She sent* **them** *to* **us**
After prepositions	*It's for* **me** *• It was written by* **her**

● **Determinative possessive pronouns:** *my, your, his, her, its, our, their*

Before noun	*That's* **my** *pullover • Do you like* **their** *dog?*
Before *–ing*	**Her** *writing is good • I can't stand* **his** *singing*

● **Independent possessive pronouns:** *mine, yours, his, hers, its, ours, theirs*

Before verb	**Ours** *is a Volvo •* **Yours** *came last*
After verb	*Who ate* **mine**? *• Someone stole* **hers**
After preposition	*Come to* **mine** *• It's between* **theirs** *and* **ours**

● **Reflexive pronouns:** *myself, yourself, himself, herself, itself, ourselves, yourselves, themselves*

After verb	*She hurt* **herself** *• We invited* **ourselves**
After preposition	*I did it by* **myself** *• It twists around* **itself**

● **Reciprocal pronouns:** *each other, one another*

After verb	*They love* **each other** *• We slapped* **one another** *on the back*
After preposition	*They circled round* **one another** *• We looked at* **each other**

● **Demonstrative pronouns:** *this, that, these, those*

Before verb	**This** *needs freezing •* **These** *haven't been cooked*
After verb	*I want* **those** *• Can you clean* **this**?
After object pronoun	*Give me* **that** *• Who sent you* **those**?
After preposition	*Don't put it on* **that**! *• You mix it with* **this**

● **Indefinite pronouns (1):** *one, none, some, any*

Before verb	**Some** *have wings •* **One** *lives in caves •* **None** *eat sugar •* **Any** *can sing*
After verb	*I don't want* **any** *• I haven't got* **one** *• There is* **none** *• I need* **some**
Before preposition	**one** *of us •* **none** *for him •* **some** *with hair •* **any** *in the garden*

● **Indefinite pronouns (2):** *every/some/no/any + thing/one/body*

Before verb	**Everyone** *finished their food •* **Nothing** *has happened*
After verb	*I didn't see* **anything** *• I want to find* **someone**
After Preposition	*Chips with* **everything** *• There's no reduction on* **anything**

● **Interrogative pronouns:** *who, whom, what, whose*

Before verb	**Who** *found him? •* **Whose** *are these? •* **What** *did you find?*
After preposition	*To* **whom** *did you send it? • It's made from* **what**?

● **Relative pronouns:** *who, whom, which, that*

After noun, before verb	*the man* **who** *stole it • my chair,* **which** *collapsed*
After noun, before pronoun	*Mr. Fag,* **who(m)** *I never met • the cake* **that** *he ate*
After preposition	*the man with* **whom** *she travelled • a house in* **which** *he lived*

Orientation

● Time: present reference point

Present	I'm eating **right now** • I'm busy **at the moment** She's not here **today** • What are you up to **this week**?
Past	**At that time** I was in Canada • I noticed her just **then** The hamster died **yesterday** • He moved here **last year**
Past to present	I have **already** cut the lettuce • She has **just** gone to bed We haven't seen them **since** Friday • Is it ready **yet**?
Future	**Tomorrow**? Okay, I'll see you **then** • What's on **tonight**? Showers are expected **next week** • I'll be finished **in two hours**

● Time: past reference point

Past with past	They were chatting **when** we came in • I went to bed **when** I got home **While** he was phoning, burglars broke into the house
Past then past	She watered the roses and **then** pricked the lawn He laid the turf on the virgin lawn. **After that** he sat in a garden chair
Past before past	**When** I had finished, I had a well-deserved drink She called him **as soon as** she had got up

● Time: future reference point

Future with future	We'll be sitting in the garden **when** you come She'll be in Australia **while** I'm on my way to India
Future then future	We'll get the chairs and **then** we'll see about the table I'll cook the onions. **After that** I'll eat them
Future before future	I'll have gone home **by the time** you have finished I'll make some tea **before** I do the washing

● Place: relative to speaker's location

Proximity	The Brands are **here** • The needle was just **here** a minute ago
Distance	Your bicycle is over **there** **There**'s the postman!
Position	**To my left** I could see the lodge • **Below** lay the boiling sea
Movement	When are you **going**? • I **came** to England seven months ago They say they're **bringing** a cake • Can you **take** this plate away? • **Fetch**!

● Place: relative to listener's location

Movement	I'll **come** as soon as I can • Can I **bring** a friend?

● Place: indefinite location

Proximate space	The spatula must be **somewhere** • I can't see it **anywhere**
Unbounded space	**Nowhere** on earth will you find such geraniums The asteroid could be **anywhere** by now

● Interpersonal

Individual	**I** am the owner and **you** are the tenant • Can **you** give it to **me**?
Group	**We** have decided to reward all of **you** • **(You)** tell **us**
External	Did you see **them**? • **She** has left **me**

● Pointing/indicating

Proximity: named entity	**This** island's mine! • **These** bonbons are absolutely delicious.
Proximity: unnamed entity	Here, take a look at **this** • I'm quite interested in **these**
Distance: named entity	**That** man's wearing his mother's hat • **These** beans should be thrown away
Distance: unnamed entity	Take **that** out of here • Could I have a look at **those**?
Discourse	**That**'s not what I meant • **This** is the key point **The former** has striped wings; **the latter** has a large thorax

Adjectives: Common Categories

Aberration	*freakish • aberrant • anomalous • unusual • abnormal • eccentric • weird*
Age	*old • young • ancient • new • antique • youthful • middle-aged*
Animal similes	*elephantine • wolflike • bearlike • catty • foxy • fishy • mousy • ratty*
Approximation	*youngish • reddish • tallish • fullish • softish • oldish*
Attraction	*sexy • fit • yummy • gorgeous • lovely • cracking*
Build	*fat • tall • broad-shouldered • slim • well-built • petite • skinny • squat*
Character	*taciturn • mendacious • dastardly • cunning • intense • generous*
Classification	*personal • internal • biochemical • leguminous • geographical • social*
Colour	*green • red • blue • yellowish • silver • golden • purple • ochre • maroon • black*
Comfort	*comfortable • soft • rough • spiky • lumpy • bumpy*
Density	*crowded • sparse • full • empty • dense • packed*
Dimension	*deep • high • wide • long • broad • narrow • elongated • tall*
Emphasis	*perfect • utter • total • complete • absolute • thundering • bloody*
Energy	*vigorous • half-hearted • energetic • frantic • languid • laid-back*
Facial features	*angular • pointed • cleft • hooked • full • rosy • craggy • beetling • goofy*
Frequency	*frequent • occasional • rare • usual • regular • daily • hourly*
Hair	*bushy • wavy • curly • straight • mousy • unkempt • unmanageable*
Honesty	*honest • frank • straightforward • dishonest • shifty • deceitful • hypocritical*
Impression	*entertaining • awful • brilliant • superb • revolting • boring • wicked*
Intelligence	*bright • sharp • intelligent • cunning • stupid • thick • brainless*
Intensity	*fantastic • incredible • extraordinary • terrible • abysmal • awful • appalling*
Lines	*parallel • zig-zag • winding • curved • broken • thin • dotted • continuous*
Luminosity	*bright • shiny • sparkling • luminous • glowing • transparent*
Manner	*sheepish • conciliatory • brisk • careful • watchful • supercilious • relaxed*
Mood	*angry • depressed • cheerful • upset • morose • reflective • hysterical*
Noise	*loud • noisy • piercing • faint • low • high-pitched • inaudible • thumping*
Plasticity	*ductile • malleable • flexible • rigid • brittle • bendy • squashy*
Quality	*good • bad • hopeless • crap • middling • mediocre • so-so • foul • beastly • revolting*
Reality	*real • solid • unreal • supernatural • surreal • otherworldly • fantastic*
Regularity	*regular • straight • higgledy-piggledy • disordered • crooked*
Sentiment	*sugary • sentimental • gushing • soupy • sickly • sickmaking • cheesy*
Shape	*round • hexagonal • star-shaped • triangular • irregular • rectangular*
Significance	*important • significant • seminal • piddling • trivial • insignificant • humble*
Size	*big • large • huge • enormous • gigantic • massive • small • little • tiny • microscopic*
Speed	*fast • slow • speedy • sluggish • swift*
Surface	*rough • smooth • angular • pockmarked • rutted • craggy • shiny*
Taste	*pungent • spicy • bland • salty • bitter • sweet • sour*
Temperament	*cheerful • gloomy • miserable • aggressive • bad-tempered • hysterical*
Texture	*hard • soft • squishy • semi-liquid • solid • chewy • spongy*
Viscosity	*runny • sticky • viscous • fluid • congealed • jelly-like*

Compound Adjectives

Adjective + Verb + -*ing*	*good-looking • foul-smelling • sweet-tasting • friendly-seeming*
Adjective + past participle	*remote-controlled • thick-sliced • hard-edged • soft-focussed*
Adjective + past participle of converted noun	*big-headed • red-haired • kind-hearted • blue-eyed • knock kneed short-sighted • rosy-cheeked • flat-bottomed*
Adverb + adverb	*well-off • badly-off • hard-up*
Adverb + Verb + -*ing*	*soundly-sleeping • hard-working • fast-running • slow-moving*
Adverb + past participle	*well-known • well-dressed • badly-behaved • scantily-clad • well-spent warmly-welcomed • much-appreciated • ill-considered*
Adverb + adjective	*all-American • half-Chinese • partly Nigerian*
Determiner + past participle of converted noun	*many-sided • two-footed • half-hearted • no-handed*
***first/second/third* + noun**	*firsthand • second-class • third-rate*
***front/back* + noun**	*frontline • backroom • front-desk*
***half* + past participle**	*half-hearted • half-eaten • half-finished • half-baked • half-cut*
Nationality + past participle	*British-born • German-based • French-made • Russian-distilled*
Noun + adjective	*top-secret • world-famous • streetwise • user-friendly*
Noun + adverb	*head-on • hands-off • bone-in*
Noun + -*free*	*gluten-free • fat-free • worry-free • waste-free • interest-free*
Noun + past participle	*hand-crafted • machine-made • oven-cooked • leather-bound*
Noun + past participle of converted noun	*lion-hearted • humpbacked • fork-tongued • velvet-coated*
Noun + -*proof*	*waterproof • childproof • bullet-proof • bullshit-proof*
Past participle + adverb	*built-up • run-down • laid-out • fed-up • laid-back • cut-out*
Past participle of converted noun + adverb	*souped-up • handed-down • backed-up • boxed-in*
Past participle + noun	*cut-price • wrought-iron • woven-wool • shot-silk*
Past participle + preposition	*unheard-of • unlooked-for • hoped-for • sewn-in*
Preposition + noun	*off-peak • on-song • in-form • out-of-work • off-piste • off-book*
Pronoun + preposition	*all-out • one-off • all-in • all-round • one-up*

Comparatives

● Forms of comparative adjectives

Doubled consonant	y → ier	more and less with longer adjectives	Irregular forms
big → bigger hot → hotter fat → fatter thin → thinner	happy → happier early → earlier silly → sillier hungry → hungrier	more intelligent less expensive more thoughtful less absurd	good → better bad → worse far → farther far → further

● Comparisons using than

Big difference

Horses are	much	bigger	than	dogs
Dogs are	far	more intelligent	than	cats
Fred is	a lot	happier	than	he used to be
Brazil is	considerably	hotter	than	France
Joe is	somewhat	less ambitious	than	Kate

Small difference

Norwich is	not much	bigger	than	Cambridge
Doughnuts are	slightly	more expensive	than	Danish pastries
Steel is	a bit	harder	than	copper
John is	hardly any	taller	than	Joanna

● Comparatives using as (adjective) as

Negation

It's	not	as sunny as it was yesterday

Big difference

Our house is	not nearly	as big as theirs
Frankie is	nowhere near	as talented as Vicky
This book is	nothing like	as good as the last one I read

Small difference

He's	almost	as tall as his father
Spain is	nearly	as big as France
This knife is	not quite	as useful as that one

Approximation

Frogs are	about	as intelligent as mice
A jaguar is	roughly	as fast as a leopard
This book is	approximately	as heavy as a loaf of bread

Exactness

The Cam is	half	as wide as the Ouse
Tracy is	twice	as intelligent as Roger
Edinburgh is	three times	as far as Lincoln

● Comparatives using the same (noun) as

These boots are nearly the same	size	as John's
Anne is about the same	weight	as Margaret
The Chrysler Building is not the same	height	as the Empire State Building
Our patio is nowhere near the same	length	as theirs
This table is not nearly the same	width	as that one
My book is approximately the same	thickness	as yours
Loch Ness is almost the same	depth	as Lake Baikal
This custard is roughly the same	density	as mercury
This pie is virtually the same	price	as that one

Superlatives

• Forms of superlative adjectives

Double consonant	-y changing to -iest	most and least with longer adjectives	Irregular forms	
the biggest	the happiest	the most intelligent	good	the best
the hottest	the earliest	the least expensive	bad	the worst
the fattest	the silliest	the most thoughtful	far	the farthest
the thinnest	the hungriest	the least absurd	far	the furthest

• With adverbials

	Big difference	
These apples are	by far	the ripest
This car is	easily	the most expensive

	Small difference	
This wine is	just about	the tastiest
He was	only just	the fastest

• With prepositional phrases

		Place
Russia is	the biggest country	in the world
He is	the fastest sprinter	on earth
Birmingham has	the friendliest people	in England
Chick peas are	the tastiest pulses	in the larder

		Collective entities
She is	the most accomplished player	in the team
He is	the worst student	in the class
He is	the most determined robber	in the gang

		Plural entities
This novel is	the best	of the bunch
She was	the least inspiring speaker	of the lot
Bartok is	the most original	of all modern composers

		Time period
Goya was	the most disturbing artist	of his era
Einstein was	the greatest scientist	of the 20th century
Confucius was	the most influential philosopher	of all time

• With relative clauses

		Present Perfect
'Guernica' is	the most impressive painting	(that) I have seen this year
This is	the worst coffee	(that) I have ever tasted

		Modal
These are	the biggest radishes	(that) you will find anywhere
He has	the bushiest eyebrows	(that) you can imagine

• With non-finite clauses

		Infinitive
She is	the youngest ever horse	to take part in this race
Last winter was	the coldest	to have hit us this century

		-ing
This gadget is	the handiest thing	going
He's	the best striker	currently playing

© Peter Bendall 2010

19

Prefixes

Types	Nouns	Adjectives	Verbs
Absence	*non*-occurrence	*a*political • *non*-alcoholic	
Across		*trans*national *trans*oceanic	*trans*ship
Against	*anti*-abortionist *counter*-revolution *contra*flow	*anti*-bacterial *counter*-intuitive	*counter*act
Apart	*dis*unity	*dis*placed	*dis*entangle
Before and after	*ex*-president • *fore*shore *ante*-meridian	*pre*-classical • *post*-war	*fore*warn • *post*date
Between/among	*inter*play	*inter*national	*inter*weave • *inter*mingle
Beyond	*para*psychology	*para*normal	*para*glide
Direction		*anti*-clockwise	
Distance	*tele*pathy	*tele*visual • *tele*pathic	*tele*vise
Division	*bi*focals	*bi*-monthly • *twice*-yearly	*bi*sect • *tri*sect
Excess/insufficiency	*over*spill	*over*cooked	*under*estimate
Extent	*half*-light	*semi*-naked • *part*-Irish *mid*-priced	*semi*-retire
Extreme quality	*ultra*sound • *super*woman	*hyper*real • *super*cool *extra*-crispy • *sub*-human	*super*heat
Extreme quantity or size	*mini*skirt • *micro*tone *mega*ton • *hyper*market	*mega*-rich	*hyper*ventilate
Increase/decrease	*up*swing	*down*cast	*up*grade • *down*size *en*large • *em*bitter
Level	*hypo*nym	*above*-mentioned	*super*impose • *sub*-contract
Negation	*un*viability • *im*patience *il*legality • *in*solubility *ir*regularity • *dis*placement	*un*suitable • *ig*noble *im*possible • *il*logical *in*exact • *ir*responsible *dis*agreeable • *ab*normal	*dis*regard *dis*place *dis*agree
Outer/inner layer	*over*shoes • *under*wear *under*coat	*in*laid	*over*lay
Outside	*extra*position	*extra*terrestrial	*extra*dite
Plurality	*multi*-millionaire *tri*-centenary	*di*atomic • *penta*tonic	*multi*-task
Rank	*arch*bishop • *pro*-consul *vice*-principal		
Removal/reversal	*un*doing	*un*fastened	*de*frost • *dis*place • *un*tie
Repetition	*triple* Salchow	*double*-dotted	*re*trace • *re*tie
Self	*auto*-correction *self*-denial	*self*-denying	*self*-denigrate
Singularity	*uni*cycle • *mono*plane	*uni*-cellular	
Together	*co*-worker	*co*-educational	*co*-operate
Under	*infra*structure	*infra*red • *sub*-standard	
Within	*intra*net	*intra*-departmental	*en*fold
Wrongness	*mal*formation *mal*distribution	*ill*-advised • *ill*-defined	*mis*place • *mis*pronounce

Suffixes: derivation

● Noun to adjective

-able	charity → charitable • profit → profitable • fashion → fashionable • reason → reasonable
-al	tradition → traditional • region → regional • occasion → occasional • accident → accidental profession → professional • intention → intentional • globe → global • centre → central
-ary	literature → literary • caution → cautionary
-ate	affection → affectionate • extortion → extortionate • fortune → fortunate
-ed	conceit → conceited • timber → timbered • floor → floored
-en	silk → silken • hemp → hempen • lump → lumpen
-etic	empathy → empathetic • apathy → apathetic • sympathy → sympathetic
-ful and -less	faith → faithful/less • harm → harmful/less • thought → thoughtful/less colour → colourful/less • pain → painful/less • use → useful/less • care → careful/less
-ful not –less	master → masterful • plenty → plentiful • stress → stressful • skill → skilful delight → delightful • man → manful • waste → wasteful • peace → peaceful
-ial	territory → territorial • manor → manorial • manager → managerial commerce → commercial • residence → residential • secretary → secretarial
-ic	irony → ironic • moron → moronic • hero → heroic • colon → colonic
-ical	geography → geographical • history → historical • politics → political
-ish	child → childish • amateur → amateurish • tiger → tigerish
-ive	aggression → aggressive • excess → excessive • authority → authoritative secret → secretive • mass → massive
-less not –ful	penny → penniless • speech → speechless • point → pointless • end → endless heart → heartless • effort → effortless • time → timeless • sleep → sleepless
-ly	time → timely • life → lively • love → lovely • friend → friendly
-ous	danger → dangerous • mystery → mysterious • melody → melodious • envy → envious nerve → nervous • luxury → luxurious • humour → humorous • anxiety → anxious
-some	whole → wholesome • tooth → toothsome
-y	salt → salty • wind → windy • sex → sexy • oil → oily • juice → juicy • peach → peachy

● Noun to verb

-ate	captive → captivate • difference → differentiate • assassin → assassinate
-en	height → heighten • length → lengthen • strength → strengthen
-ify	terror → terrify • horror → horrify • mystery → mystify • peace → pacify
-ise	sympathy → sympathise • maximum → maximise • terror → terrorise
Ø	bottle → bottle • spoon → spoon • finger → finger • man → man • shop → shop

● Adjective to noun

-ance	arrogant → arrogance • tolerant → tolerance • important → importance • distant → distance
-cy	supreme → supremacy • illiterate → illiteracy • numerate → numeracy
-dom	wise → wisdom • free → freedom • bored → boredom
-ence	eloquent → eloquence • permanent → permanence • patient → patience • absent → absence
-iety	anxious → anxiety • sober → sobriety • notorious → notoriety
-ity + no spellingchange	normal → normality • stupid → stupidity • insipid → insipidity • similar → similarity complex → complexity • personal → personality • real → reality • popular → popularity
-ity + spelling change	mature → maturity • generous → generosity • diverse → diversity objective → objectivity • prosperous → prosperity • immune → immunity
-ness	happy → happiness • conspicuous → conspicuousnesss • blind → blindness • stiff → stiffness eager → eagerness • thorough → thoroughness • conscious → consciousness
-tion	desperate → desperation • considerate → consideration
-y	accurate → accuracy • jealous → jealousy • frequent → frequency

Suffixes (continued)

● Adjective to verb

-en	wide → widen • red → redden • dark → darken • fresh → freshen • sweet → sweeten
	bright → brighten • soft → soften • flat → flatten • sad → sadden • worse → worsen
-ify	simple → simplify • pure → purify • clear → clarify
-ise	intellectual → intellectualise • visual → visualise • general → generalise
	modern → modernise • special → specialise • familiar → familiarise

● Verb to noun

-age	break → breakage • post → postage • wreck → wreckage • cover → coverage
-al	appraise → appraisal • refuse → refusal • defer → deferral • dismiss → dismissal
-ance/-ancy	perform → performance • appear → appearance • expect → expectancy • rely → reliance
	disturb → disturbance • tolerate → tolerance • endure → endurance • annoy → annoyance
-ant	ruminate → ruminant • supplicate → supplicant • apply → applicant • assist → assistant
-cess	succeed → success • exceed → excess • proceed → process
-ence/-ency	defend → defence • offend → offence • obey → obedience • persist → persistence
	differ → difference • precede → precedence • emerge → emergency
-er/-or	run → runner • teach → teacher • bite → biter • lead → leader • act → actor
-iour	behave → behaviour • save → saviour
-ment	encourage → encouragement • equip → equipment • enjoy → enjoyment
	develop → development • refresh → refreshment • require → requirement
	commit → commitment • embarrass → embarrassment • settle → settlement
Ø	fear → fear • hope → hope • attack → attack • laugh → laugh • call → call
-ption	receive → reception • deceive → deception • conceive → conception
	subscribe → subscription • inscribe → inscription
-sion	decide → decision • expand → expansion • elide → elision • excise → excision
-ssion	submit → submission • commit → commission • permit → permission
-tion	suggest → suggestion • pronounce → pronunciation • substitute → substitution
	prepare → preparation • adapt → adaptation • publish → publication • vary → variation
-ure	please → pleasure • close → closure • seize → seizure

● Verb to adjective

-able/-ible	change → changeable • excite → excitable • eat → eatable • play → playable
	pay → payable • irritate → irritable • regret → regrettable • consider → considerable
-ant	ruminate → ruminant • expect → expectant • malign → malignant
-ed	tire → tired • restrict → restricted • divide → divided • interest → interested
-en/-n	break → broken • freeze → frozen • prove → proven • tear → torn • know → known
-ent	appear → apparent • abhor → abhorrent • confide → confident • insist → insistent
-ful	dread → dreadful • forget → forgetful • resent → resentful • harm → harmful
-inct	extinguish → extinct • distinguish → distinct
-ing	fascinate → fascinating • bore → boring • exhilarate → exhilarating
-ive	persuade → persuasive • compete → competitive • attract → attractive
	compete → competitive • express → expressive • support → supportive
-ous	blaspheme → blasphemous • ridicule → ridiculous
-tory	supervise → supervisory • condemn → condemnatory • prepare → preparatory
-y	run → runny • stuff → stuffy • sneer → sneery • weep → weepy • creep → creepy

● Noun to noun

-dom	star → stardom • king → kingdom • martyr → martyrdom
-ful	scoop → scoopful • mouth → mouthful • spoon → spoonful • cup → cupful
-hood	brother → brotherhood • nation → nationhood • parent → parenthood
-ian	comedy → comedian • tragedy → tragedian • mathematics → mathematician
-ist	science → scientist • hygiene → hygienist • sex → sexist • physics → physicist
-ship	censor → censorship • friend → friendship • court → courtship • fellow → fellowship

　　　　　　　　　　© Peter Bendall 2010

Dynamic verbs: common categories

Action of light	shine • reflect • glare • dazzle • glimmer • glow
Action of water	saturate • drench • soak • erode
Active perception	listen • watch • taste • smell
Agentive change of state	classify • widen • enlarge • kill • fill • empty • reduce
Amusement	laugh • giggle • snigger • titter • smile
Animal noise	bleat • cackle • bark • squeak • low • roar • grunt
Appearance/disappearance	appear • disappear • vanish • dissipate • melt
Aqueous change of state	evaporate • condense • boil • freeze
Aqueous movement	surge • swell • ripple • break • overflow • bubble
Articulation	enunciate • mumble • lisp • murmur • stammer • stutter
Becoming	go • get • grow • turn • fall • become
Bodily motion	go • run • stagger • limp • fly • gallop • hobble • leap • march
Burning	burn • scorch • blaze • smoulder • scald
Capture	catch • trap • snare • capture • hook
Change of level	fall • rise • increase • decrease • fluctuate
Change of state	deteriorate • cool • break • ossify • die • freeze
Collection	harvest • pick • reap • collect • mow • glean
Commencement/Conclusion	begin • start • commence • initiate • finish • end • conclude
Compulsion	force • persuade • make • compel • oblige
Congelation	congeal • solidify • curdle • freeze • set
Cooking	fry • boil • scramble • poach • bake • roast • coddle
Creation	create • build • make • form • construct • mould
Creation	make • build • erect • compose • sketch • cook • construct
Crepitation	snap • crackle • pop • sizzle
Crime	burgle • smuggle • pilfer • mug • rape • assault
Cutting	cut • chop • carve • slice • dissect • cleave • trim
Destruction	destroy • demolish • obliterate • crush
Discovery	find • discover • locate • pinpoint
Dissolution	melt • dissolve • thaw
Distortion	twist • distort • squash • contort
Ditransitive	give • send • bring • take • pass • promise • tell • offer
Division	cut • divide • separate • split • share
Emotional reaction	laugh • cry • weep • sigh • rage
Encapsulation	wrap • enfold • encapsulate • bundle • bury • enclose
Encroachment	encroach • invade • trespass
Event	happen • occur • take place
Excretion	urinate • defecate • vomit • sweat • bleed • lactate
Explosion	erupt • explode • burst • bang
Expropriation	confiscate • deprive • appropriate • expropriate • withdraw
Facial expression	grin • wink • frown • sneer • grimace • smile
Financial dealing	bet • invest • recoup • gamble • profit • swindle • cheat
Fluidity	trickle • pour • gush • flood • spurt • drip
Frictionless movement	slide • slither • slip • float
Hurried movement	rush • hurry • hasten • gobble • gulp
Ignition/extinguishment	light • ignite • extinguish • snuff • douse

Dynamic verbs (continued)

Ingestion	*eat • drink • swallow • devour • gulp • gobble • sip*
Interaction	*negotiate • deal • interview • bargain*
Internal bodily processes	*digest • ingest • circulate • absorb*
Interrogation	*ask • inquire • interrogate • demand • query*
Involuntary bodily noise	*fart • belch • rumble • creak • burp*
Loss	*lose • mislay • misplace • forfeit*
Machine noise	*tick • whirr • clank • wheeze*
Machine/equipment verbs	*phone • cycle • parachute • ski*
Mental processes	*consider • deliberate • ponder • contemplate • decide*
Movement in relation to a point	*arrive • reach • depart • leave • pass • return*
Movement in relation to a volume	*enter • leave • exit • quit*
Movement in relation to an area	*cross • traverse • enter • leave • pass • quit*
Movement of bodies (transitive)	*push • pull • drag • heave • lift • drop*
Movement of bodies (intransitive)	*slam • heave • crash • sway • crumple • collapse • wobble*
Nasal/buccal noise	*snort • sniff • snore • wheeze • pant*
Pain	*hurt • throb • ache • stab*
Reaction to pain	*groan • moan • scream • shriek*
Percussion	*hit • thump • bash • whack • smack • knock • bang • smite*
Performance by utterance	*declare • swear • warn • promise • suggest • propose*
Permission	*permit • allow • let • tolerate*
Perusal	*observe • inspect • check • examine • peruse*
Physical reaction	*shiver • shudder • sweat • sneeze • cough • swoon • faint*
Precipitation	*rain • snow • hail • sleet • drizzle*
Puncturation	*prick • cut • spear • pierce • puncture*
Random movement	*fiddle • twiddle • wander • twitch • fidget*
Regulation	*control • regulate • calibrate • synchronise*
Reporting	*say • tell • report • relay*
Response	*answer • respond • reply • react • retort*
Retrospection	*remember • recall • regret • recollect*
Revolution	*turn • revolve • swivel • spin*
Sadness	*cry • weep • sob • snivel • sigh*
Sibilance	*hiss • whisper • rustle*
Slow movement	*loiter • linger • traipse • trudge • crawl*
Social intercourse	*talk • chat • communicate • speak • say • tell • participate*
Soufflation	*blow • drift • puff • waft*
Sporting actions	*score • pass • hit • kick • drive • cut • bowl • throw*
Stance	*sit • stand • lie • crouch • lean • slouch*
Surface alteration	*scrape • scratch • scuff • score • ruffle • shave*
Transaction	*give • receive • buy • sell*
Transport of goods (transitive)	*transport • move • ship • remove • carry*
Transport of people (intransitive)	*drive • ride • travel • sail • fly*
Understanding	*understand • comprehend • glean • follow*
Unsystematic movement	*swish • swipe • swat • flail • stagger*
Utterance	*speak • shout • mutter • whisper • burble • scream • sing • hum*
Victory/defeat	*win • lose • overcome • thrash • submit • prevail*
Ways of killing and injuring	*stab • strangle • suffocate • crush • poison • shoot • hang*

Stative verbs

Agreement	I completely **agree** with you • He **accepts** that he was wrong
Appearance	He **seems** quite capable • They **appeared** to be drunk
Capacity	This jug **holds** two litres • This camera **takes** four AA batteries
Cause	His insecurity **stems** from his childhood • Insecurity **underlies** his ambition
Cognition	I **know** you're tired • She didn't **recognise** me • I **forget** his name • I **agree**
Composition	The property **comprises** two dwellings • The class **consists** of twelve students
Connection	The new road **links** Bedford and Luton • This lead **connects** to the modem
Deficiency	He **lacks** patience • The book **doesn't include** an index
Desire	I **want** that dandelion • I **wish** I could swim
Duration	The film **lasts** for three hours • It **takes** ages to get there
Entailment	Being a teacher **involves** marking • The work **entails** a lot of close inspection
Equivalence	Nine times eight **equals** 72 • 5 plus 7 **makes** a dozen
Existence	Sloths **live** in trees • Does life **exist** in outer space?
Feature	She **has** a long chin • The property **features** an unusual living room
Sense impression	It **tastes** of plastic • It **feels** slimy • Her voice **sounds** distant
Interpersonal	She **sympathises** with you • He **doesn't respect** anybody's feelings
Location	A hedge **surrounds** the garden • A fence **divides** the two properties
Meaning	'Pulchritude' **means** 'beauty' • What does her behaviour **signify**?
Measure	It **weighs** two tons • The land **measures** 30m x 40m
Negative feeling	I **loathe** pilchards • She **hates** dust • He **dreads** the rainy season • I **detest** drivers
Origin	She **comes** from Geneva • This material **originates** in Turkey
Perception	I **smell** dumplings • Did you **hear** that? • I **can't see** the board
Performance	I **declare** this meeting open • I **name** this ship 'Blue Swallow'
Permanence	His body **lies** in Histon churchyard • The tower **has stood** there for centuries
Positive feeling	We **like** your plum tree • I **love** garlic • She **adores** her new pony
Possession	It **belongs** to me • She **owns** the whole estate • He **has** no money
Preference	They **prefer** trekking • I **favour** the red one
Regulation	Rule 34b **states** that fish may not be caught • The notice **says** No Entry
Relation	It **depends** on Joe • It **suits** you • It **doesn't fit** him • It **doesn't concern** you
Superfluity	The audience **exceeds** capacity • It **surpasses** every other contemporary building
Survival	Nothing **remains** of the chapel • At least her sense of humour **has survived**
Symbolism	Fish **symbolise** insouciance • MP **stands for** Member of Parliament

Irregular verb forms

● Verbs with a regular and irregular form

burn	burned	burned	spell	spelled	spelled
	burnt	burnt		spelt	spelt
dream	dreamed	dreamed	spill	spilled	spilled
	dreamt	dreamt		spilt	spilt
learn	learned	learned	light	lighted	lighted
	learnt	learnt		lit	lit
leap	leaped	leaped			
	leapt	leapt			

● Change of vowel in past form; past participle same as base form

come	came	come	become	became	become

● Regular past form; -n/-en past participle

mow	mowed	mown	shear	sheared	shorn
sew	sewed	sown	shave	shaved	shaven
show	showed	shown	swell	swelled	swollen
sow	sowed	sown	prove	proved	proven

● Base form same as past form; -en past participle

beat	beat	beaten

● Change of vowel: same vowel in past and past participle; -en/-n/-ne past participle

choose	chose	chosen	forget	forgot	forgotten
steal	stole	stolen	speak	spoke	spoken
weave	wove	woven	break	broke	broken
freeze	froze	frozen	bear	bore	borne
(a)wake	(a)woke	(a)woken	tear	tore	torn
bite	bit	bitten	wear	wore	worn
hide	hid	hidden	swear	swore	sworn
tread	trod	trodden	lie	lay	lain

● Change of vowel in past and past participle; -en/-n past participle

ride	rode	ridden	strive	strove	striven
smite	smote	smitten	fly	flew	flown
write	wrote	written	rise	rose	risen
drive	drove	driven	arise	arose	arisen

● Same vowel in base form and past participle; change of vowel in past; -en/-n past participle

give	gave	given	slay	slew	slain
forgive	forgave	forgiven	shake	shook	shaken
bid	bade	bidden	take	took	taken
forbid	forbade	forbidden	forsake	forsook	forsaken
fall	fell	fallen	blow	blew	blown
eat	ate	eaten	grow	grew	grown
draw	drew	drawn	know	knew	known
see	saw	seen	throw	threw	thrown

● Change of vowel; same form in past and past participle

dig	dug	dug	seek	sought	sought
hear	heard	heard	think	thought	thought
hold	held	held	fight	fought	fought
leave	left	left	buy	bought	bought
shine	shone	shone	bring	brought	brought
slide	slid	slid	catch	caught	caught
strike	struck	struck	wreak	wrought	wrought

Irregular verb forms (continued)

● Change of vowel; same form in past and past participle (continued)

speed	sped	sped	teach	taught	taught
sleep	slept	slept	meet	met	met
keep	kept	kept	get	got	got
creep	crept	crept	shoot	shot	shot
weep	wept	wept	lose	lost	lost
sweep	swept	swept	feel	felt	felt
shoe	shod	shod	kneel	knelt	knelt
win	won	won	bind	bound	bound
cling	clung	clung	find	found	found
sling	slung	slung	wind	wound	wound
sting	stung	stung	grind	ground	ground
swing	swung	swung	breed	bred	bred
fling	flung	flung	flee	fled	fled
string	strung	strung	lead	led	led
wring	wrung	wrung	read	read	read
hang	hung	hung	lean	leant	leant
sell	sold	sold	mean	meant	meant
tell	told	told	sit	sat	sat
stride	strode	strode	spit	spat	spat
stand	stood	stood	stick	stuck	stuck
understand	understood	understood	say	said	said

● Change of consonant; same form in past and past participle

build	built	built	bend	bent	bent
deal	dealt	dealt	lend	lent	lent
make	made	made	send	sent	sent
pay	paid	paid	spend	spent	spent
lay	laid	laid	have	had	had

● Change of vowel; *a* in past, *u* in past participle

begin	began	begun	ring	rang	rung
swim	swam	swum	sing	sang	sung
drink	drank	drunk	spring	sprang	sprung
sink	sank	sunk	run	ran	run
shrink	shrank	shrunk	spin	span	spun
stink	stank	stunk			

● Same three forms

fit	fit	fit	bid	bid	bid
hit	hit	hit	rid	rid	rid
quit	quit	quit	shed	shed	shed
slit	slit	slit	cast	cast	cast
split	split	split	broadcast	broadcast	broadcast
bet	bet	bet	burst	burst	burst
let	let	let	hurt	hurt	hurt
set	set	set	thrust	thrust	thrust
cut	cut	cut	cost	cost	cost
put	put	put	spread	spread	spread
shut	shut	shut			

● Thoroughly irregular verbs

be	was/were	been	go	went	gone
do	did	done			

Primary auxiliaries: *Do, Be* and *Have*

● *Do* with base form: questions

Present: *I, you, we, they + do*	**Do** I snore? • **Do** you like tulips? • **Do** we sit here? • **Do** they eat meat?
Present *he, she, it + does*	**Does** he smoke? • **Does** she ever come on time? • What **does** it do?
Past: All persons + *did*	**Did** I say that? • **Did** she get there on time? • **Did** we invite them?

● *Do* with base form: negatives

Present: *I, you, we, they + don't*	I **don't** agree • You **don't** care • We **don't** smoke • They **don't** know
Present: *he, she, it + doesn't*	He **doesn't** drink • She **doesn't** want to know • It **doesn't** matter
Past: All persons + *didn't*	I **didn't** understand • You **didn't** feed it • We **didn't** get back in time

● *Do* with base form: emphatic

Present	You **do** look nice! • She **does** dance well! • They **do** make a lot of noise
Past	They **did** eat a lot! • The Greeks **did** know about atoms

● *Be* with *-ing*

Present: *I + am*	**Am** I repeating myself? • I **am** waiting, Martin • I**'m not** playing
Present: *you, we, they + are*	You**'re** being silly • We **aren't** sinking • They**'re** batting
Present: *he, she, it + is*	**Is** she working? • He**'s** dancing • It**'s** burning
Past: *I, he, she, it + was*	I **was** painting • She **wasn't** eating much • It **was** wagging its tail
Past: *you, we, they + were*	You **were** complaining • We **were** killing ourselves • They **were** smiling

● *Be* with past participle

Present: *I + am*	I **am** visited by the Gruffs every Thursday • **Am** I excused?
Present: *you, we, they + are*	You **are** known to the police • We **are** not listed
Present: *he, she, it + is*	He**'s** tired • She**'s** not dressed • **Is** it broken?
Past: *I, he, she, it + was*	It **was** opened • She **was** distressed • He **was** slumped on the floor
Past: *you, we, they + were*	You **were** missed • We **weren't** noticed • **Were** they caught?

● Modal + *be* + *-ing*

All persons + *be*	She might **be** going out • They should **be** arriving • It can't **be** snowing

● *Have* with past participle

Present: *I, you, we, they + have*	I**'ve** lost my coat • You**'ve** cut yourself • We **haven't** been here long
Present: *he, she, it + has*	She**'s** gone away • He **has** won the lottery • It **hasn't** snowed lately
Past: All persons	We **had** just got up • He **had** fallen over • They **had** overpaid

● Modal + *have* + past participle

All persons + *have*	We could **have** won • She might **have** apologised • I can't **have** failed

● *Have* + *been* + *-ing*

Present: *I, you, we, they + have*	I**'ve been** sleeping badly • We **haven't been** sailing yet
Present: *he, she, it + has*	It**'s been** hailing • **Has** she **been** ski-ing? • He **hasn't been** drinking
Past: All persons + *had*	They **had been** hiking • He **had been** building a new shed

● Modal + *have* + *been* + *-ing*

All persons + modal + *have been*	She'll **have been** riding • They might **have been** looking for something

● Modal + *have* + *been* + past participle

All persons + modal + *have been*	He should **have been** sent off • You must **have been** surprised

Uses of Modal Verbs

Use	Example
Ability	*I **can** do long division • She **could** play the oboe when she was five*
Absolute obligation	*You **must** finish by 6.00 • He **has to** get there by nine*
Advice/recommendation	*He **should** see a doctor • You **might** try yoga • You **ought to** get some sleep*
Assumption	*That **will** be the plumber • I'm sure you **will** have come across this term*
Decision	*I'll have the stewed seaweed • In that case, we **will** return the goods*
Deduction (certainty)	*He **must** be rich • They **can't** have left before 3.00*
Deduction (uncertainty)	*They **might** be in the fridge • She **may** have gone by car*
Faintheartedness	*I **daren't** go up the Eiffel Tower • We **daren't** go out in the evenings*
Hypothesis	*We **would** cancel the trip under those circumstances*
Inference	*They **should** have arrived by now • It **ought to** grow to five feet*
Intention	*I'll see you on Friday • I **shan't** do that again • I'm **going to** cook some rice*
Lack of obligation	*We **needn't** have left so early • You **don't have to** wax the floorboards*
Moral obligation	*We **ought to** go • You really **should** work harder*
Necessity	*She **needs to** get some sleep • I've **got to** go now*
Past habit 1 (no context)	*We **used to** go fishing • They **didn't use to** have a telephone*
Past habit 2 (context)	*When they lived in Paris, they **would** often go for walks by the Seine*
Permission	***Can** we have some cake now? • You **may** kiss my hand*
Persistence	*He **will** make cutting remarks • If you **will** arrive late…*
Possibility	*We **may** have a picnic on Sunday • She **could** have gone to India*
Potentiality	*The snow here **can** melt quite suddenly • He **could** be a bloody nuisance*
Prediction 1	*Tomorrow **will** be wet and windy • They **should** make it*
Prediction 2	*It's **going to** snow • They **aren't going to** turn up*
Preference	*I **would** rather go by boat • She **would** prefer to eat in her room*
Prohibition	*You **mustn't** talk in here • You **can't** come in now • They **shall** not pass*
Promise	*I'll do it first thing • We **shall** cut taxes and standardise bicycle lights*
Refusal	*She **won't** do anything I say • The cat **won't** drink its milk*
Reproach	*You **might** say thank you! • You **could** have told me earlier*
Request	***Could** you do the washing-up? • **Can** you stop that? • **Would** you wait here?*
Threat	*I'll tell your mother • We'll smash your plant pots*
Willingness	***Shall** I open the window? • I'll carry your bags • **May** I be of assistance?*

Modal	Use
can	**Ability (present), Permission, Request, Potentiality, Deduction (negative)**
could	**Ability (past), Reproach, Request, Deduction (uncertainty), Potentiality**
daren't	**Faintheartedness**
going to	**Intention, Prediction**
have to	**Obligation, Lack of obligation (negative)**
may	**Deduction (uncertainty), Permission, Possibility, Willingness**
might	**Advice/Recommendation, Deduction (uncertainty), Reproach**
must	**Absolute obligation, Deduction (certainty),**
mustn't	**Prohibition**
need	**Necessity**
needn't	**Lack of obligation, Reproach**
ought to	**Advice, Inference, Moral obligation**
shall	**Prohibition, Promise, Willingness**
should	**Advice/Recommendation, Inference, Moral obligation, Prediction**
used to	**Past Habit**
will/won't	**Assumption, Decision, Intention, Persistence, Prediction, Promise, Refusal, Threat, Willingness**
would	**Hypothesis, Past Habit, Preference, Request**

Causative verbs

Arrange for a process to be carried out (1): *have/get* + object + past participle	*I'm **having my hedge trimmed** • **Get your hair cut**!* *He **has his house repainted** every year • I've just **got my ears pierced*** *She **was having her legs waxed** when I last saw her*
Arrange for a process to be carried out (2): *get* + person + *to* infinitive	*We need to **get someone to fix** the boiler* *You'll have to **get a carpenter to put** the cupboards up* *We **got a solicitor to go** over the documents*
Be the passive victim of an action: *have/get* + object + past participle	*I **had my suitcase examined** at the airport* *He's managed **to get his bike stolen** yet again* *We've **had our fence kicked in** yet again*
Compulsion (1): *make* + person + base form; *be made* + *to* infinitive	*You can't **make me clean** my bedroom, you foul parent* *They **made us hand** over our valuables at knifepoint* *She **was made to stand** in a queue for over an hour*
Compulsion (2): *force/compel/oblige* + person + *to* infinitive	*They **forced us to lie** down with our hands on our hands* *We **were compelled to take** shelter in an old barn* *The dire economic situation **obliged her to tender** her resignation*
Direct cause (1): *cause* + person + *to* infinitive	*A scurrying mouse **caused the waiter to drop** the tray* *The pressure of the buildings has **caused the city to sink*** *Too much dust always **causes me to cough***
Direct cause (2): *cause/bring about/provoke* + eventive noun object	*Eating too fast **causes indigestion*** *The police investigation **brought about his resignation*** *So far it is not known what **provoked the explosion***
Permission (1): *let* + person + base form	*She never **lets me look** at her old photos* *If you **let me come** in, I can explain everything, Jocasta* *Uncle Geoff **lets me eat** salt and vinegar crisps*
Permission (2): *allow/permit* + person + *to* infinitive/ *be allowed/permitted* + *to* infinitive	*Would you **allow me to introduce** Mr. Tonsil, the famous surgeon?* *We cannot **permit anyone to leave** the area at this juncture* *We **were never allowed to play** that sort of game*
Persuasion: *get/persuade* someone + *to* infinitive	*Do you think we could **get Frank to bake** some currant buns?* *After a lot of argument I **got them to refund** my money* *She **persuaded me to lend** her a thousand pounds*
Provocation: *get* + past participle	*If you go around shouting like that, you'**ll get arrested*** *Don't be late too often, or you'**ll get sacked*** *If you go into that end of the ground, you're liable **to get beaten up***
Subject only partially in control of the situation: *get* + past participle	*Do you think the Blues will **get promoted**?* *I played a new variation of the Queen's Indian, but I still **got beaten*** *I'm sorry, I just **got sidetracked***

Change of state verbs

● Copular verbs — Complement

become	*president • king • director • manager • the best • clear • obvious • evident*
come	*undone • apart • to pieces • right*
fall	*ill • asleep • silent • unconscious • apart*
get	*old • hungry • angry • tired • thirsty • ill • dark • impatient • desperate*
go	*mad • crazy • bad • soft in the head • to pieces • green • rotten • senile*
grow	*old • late • dark • impatient • mysterious • cloudy*
turn	*nasty • vicious • cold • wet • windy • red • liquid*

● Transitive verbs — Object

bleach	*clothes • hair • bones • toilet*
blunt	*knife • blade • attack • enthusiasm*
cultivate	*tomatoes • vines • sense of humour • taste for modern art • friendships*
deepen	*canal • riverbed • knowledge • understanding*
enhance	*photo • colours • flavour • cooperation • understanding*
enlarge	*photo • understanding • vocabulary • knowledge*
falsify	*accounts • facts • testimony • evidence • statement*
flatten	*building • road surface • cricket pitch • curls • pastry*
heighten	*awareness • suffering • value • expression • contrast*
intensify	*flavour • taste • colour • sound • feelings*
legalise	*marijuana • reverse cycling*
lengthen/shorten	*tunnel • working hours • chain • lead • dress • trousers • lunch break*
lubricate	*engine • axles • wheels of power • sexual organs*
magnify	*photo • errors • crisis • problem • reputation*
marginalise	*ethnic minorities • small political parties*
purify	*water • mind • drugs • chemicals*
roast	*meat • parsnips • potatoes • undisciplined employees or students*
sharpen	*knife • sword • understanding • wits • outline*
soften	*attitude • resistance • morale • dough • soil*
squash	*fruit • hedgehogs • opposition • person • soft toy*
sweeten	*sauce • pudding • tea • coffee • custard*
widen	*road • path • knowledge • range of vocabulary • horizons*

Subject — ● Ergative verb

people • wine • wood • cheese	*age*
water • vegetables • volcanic lava • weather • blood	*boil*
building • edifice • biscuits • wall • confidence • civilisation • power	*crumble*
water • river • pond • lake • hands • feet • food • person	*freeze*
vegetables • trees • flowers • children • confidence • hope	*grow*
cement • mud • putty • paste • glue • attitudes	*harden*
fruit • vegetables • meat • corpses	*putrefy*
face • skin • sky • trousers	*redden*
corn • vegetables • fruit • ideas • imagination	*ripen*
fruit • vegetables • meat • wood • dead trees • carcases	*rot*
metal • bicycle • car • rails • machinery	*rust*
paint • cement • jelly • custard	*set*
clothes • image • people • confidence	*shrink*
peas • gourds • stomach • wet wood • head • seeds	*swell*

Do and *Make*

Do

Change of physical condition	the lawn • the garden • the room • the car • the carpet • the potatoes the sheets • the spaghetti • the floor • the bath
Calculation	sums • a calculation • long division • long multiplication
Effect on another person	good • someone good • someone harm • someone a favour • someone a good turn • someone an injustice • someone's head in
Enhance a part of the body	your hair • your nails • your eyelashes • your teeth • your legs
Indefinite activities	something • nothing • anything • whatever you like
Occupation	a paper round • the morning shift • an afternoon class
Performance	well • badly • okay • better • worse • your best • your worst
Process → product	tricks • duty • homework • a play • a concert • work a crossword • a puzzle • business • a deal
Process: determiner + *-ing* noun	the shopping • some cleaning • a bit of ironing • some grouting the gardening • some painting • a lot of shouting • a spot of digging
Repair/renewal	the paintwork • the gears • the chain • the blinds • the roof
Studies	an exam • a course • a diploma • a degree • geography • physics

Make

Accommodation	time for something • room for something • space for someone
Affect someone's mood	someone: happy • sad • angry • furious • mad • desperate
Amelioration	progress • a recovery • an improvement
Blame and censure	an example of someone • someone a scapegoat
Certainty	sure • certain
Change	changes • alterations • modifications
Communication	a signal • a sign • a call • a face
Compatibility	someone a good partner • a good pair
Complaint	a stink • a fuss • a song and dance about it
Confusion	someone's head spin
Creation	a cake • a meal • a good score • a noise • a nasty smell • a mess
Damage	a hole in something • a dent in something • a cut in something
Decision	a decision • a choice • a selection • your mind up
Exception	an exception • a special case
Finish	an end of something
Impression	a mark on something • an impression • an impact on someone
Inefficiency	a meal of something • a pig's ear of something a mess of something • a complete hash of it
Negative transformation	a fool of yourself • a nuisance of yourself • a pig of yourself
Noise	a sound • a noise • a row • a hullabaloo
Overcome inertia	a start • a move
Overdoing things	a fuss of someone • fun of someone
Plan	a plan • an arrangement • an appointment
Position of authority	a good captain • a reasonable manager • a hopeless boss
Reciprocal action	peace • war • love • friends • enemies • an agreement
Redundancy	someone redundant • someone unemployable • something useless
Restore to order	the bed
Sacrifice	a sacrifice • a martyr of yourself
Try	an effort • an attempt
Utterance	a speech • a proposal • a suggestion • a remark • an appeal • a point a comment • a confession • a protest • a promise • a claim • an excuse a declaration • an apology • a plea

Phrasal and prepositional verb-types

• Intransitive phrasal verbs

	Verb	Adverb
When does the plane	*take*	*off?*
Prices are continually	*going*	*up*
Don't run! You might	*fall*	*over*
I really need to	*sit*	*down*

• Transitive phrasal verbs: noun phrase before or after particle

	Verb	Direct Object	Adverb
Are you going to	*get*	*the washing*	*in?*
Could you	*put*	*the rubbish*	*out?*

	Verb	Adverb	Direct Object
Are you going to	*get*	*in*	*the washing?*
Could you	*put*	*out*	*The rubbish?*

• Transitive phrasal verbs: pronoun before particle (obligatory)

	Verb	Direct Object	Adverb
I didn't	*throw*	*it*	*out*
I'm going to	*tell*	*him*	*off*

• Intransitive prepositional verbs: inseparable verb and preposition

	Verb	Preposition	Prepositional Object
He	*takes*	*after*	*his father*
I told him to	*get*	*off*	*the wall*
Let's	*go*	*through*	*the contract*
I really	*care*	*about*	*you*

• Transitive prepositional verbs

	Verb	Direct Object	Preposition	Prepositional Object
They	*accused*	*his wife*	*of*	*shoplifting*
Don't	*make*	*a mess*	*of*	*the place*
I	*thank*	*everyone*	*for*	*their kindness*
Will you	*remind*	*her*	*of*	*her promise?*

• Intransitive phrasal-prepositional verbs

	Verb	Adverb	Preposition	Prepositional Object
She wants to	*get*	*away*	*from*	*this place*
I simply can't	*put*	*up*	*with*	*his belching*
He	*isn't*	*down*	*for*	*the trip*
He tried to	*wriggle*	*out*	*of*	*it*

• Transitive phrasal-prepositional verbs

	Verb	Direct Object	Adverb	Preposition	Prepositional Object
She needs to	*turn*	*it*	*over*	*in*	*her mind*
He can't	*put*	*it*	*across*	*to*	*the class*
I'm going to	*send*	*this form*	*round*	*to*	*the members*
I hope you're	*keeping*	*them*	*up*	*to*	*the mark*

Common phrasal verbs

● Be

Please stay in your seats until he match **is over**	has finished
Don't drink that milk – it**'s off**	has gone bad
I**'m off** to Cyprus tomorrow	I'm leaving for Cyprus
I think we**'re in for** a cold winter	We're going to have a cold winter
Are you **down for** the Oxford trip?	Are you on the list?
What **are** the adults **up to**?	What naughty things are they doing?
I can't tell you – I**'m not in on** the secret	I haven't been told the secret

● Break

I'm sorry I'm late. My car **broke down**	stopped working
The papers have gone – someone must have **broken in**	entered the premises illegally
They have **broken up**	ended their relationship
Flu has **broken out** in the south of England	started suddenly (disease, war)
The rebels have **broken off** talks with the government	ended suddenly (talks, negotiations)
The company is to be **broken up** and sold off	reduced to its constituent parts
The army has **broken through** the rebel lines	penetrated the defences

● Bring

The cold weather **brought about** his hacking cough	caused
The new manager aims to **bring in** major changes	introduce
The final scene **brought on** a general fit of weeping	provoked
He was **brought up** by his Aunt Devonia	cared for/trained (socially)
The big occasion always **brings out** the best in her	encourages
When are they **bringing out** your new pot-boiler?	publishing
You'd better **bring** the matter **up** at the next meeting	mention
We're hoping to **bring off** the deal by next Tuesday	complete (business deal0

● Call

The match has been **called off** due to a plague of moths	cancelled
The police were **called in** to deal with the situation	summoned
Shall we go and **call on** Pam?	visit
Can you **call off** your dogs?	stop them attacking
I **call on** everybody to make a big effort	appeal to
The council are **calling on** volunteers to clear away the snow	appealing to

● Come

The truth will eventually **come out**	be revealed
She **came up with** a brilliant solution	provided/produced
His work doesn't **come up to** the required standard	reach/attain
I'm having a party tonight. Why don't you **come round**?	come to my house
What time does the sun **come up**?	rise
Did anything of note **come up** at the meeting?	arise
When **do** the results **come out**?	When are they published?
I **came across** a rare first edition at the book fair	found by chance
Fred **came into** a lot of money when his aunt died	inherited
The handle **came off** in my hand	was removed inadvertently

● Cut

You'll have to **cut out** fatty foods if you want to lose weight	exclude
He hasn't **cut down** his smoking at all	reduced
Three villages have been **cut off** by the floods	isolated
The walnut tree was **cut down** because it was dangerous	felled
Do you mind if I **cut** this picture **out of** the newspaper?	remove with scissors
Cut up the carrots into cubes	cut into pieces
Can you stop **cutting in** when I'm talking?	interrupting

Common phrasal verbs (continued)

● Do

They are going to **do away with** council tax!	abolish
It's time you **did out** your room	cleaned
I'm completely **done in** after that boring lecture	exhausted
They're **doing up** the town for Christmas	decorating
Do up your buttons, Bertrand	fasten

● Fall

I hope you didn't **fall for** that story of his	innocently believe
Our holiday plans **fell through** at the last minute	became incapable of realisation
George has **fallen for** Christine, but she's not available	become romantically interested in
Demand for sugar mice **fell off** dramatically last year	diminished
He's just **fallen out with** his best friend	had a serious disagreement with
Don't climb on that wall! You'll **fall off**	lose your balance and fall

● Get

Do you think John will **get through** the statistics exam?	pass (exam, test)
Mandy and Gordon don't really **get on**	have a good relationship
It's only a slight cold – I'll soon **get over** it	recover from (illness, bad experience)
The best way to **get round** him is by giving him sweets	gently persuade him to do something
These secrets must never **get out**	be revealed
Don't open the window – the parrot will **get out**	escape
You'll never **get through** so many cream cakes, Harold	finish (food, tasks)
What time did you **get up** this morning?	arise from your bed
Mr. Robinson is **getting on for** eighty, I should think	approaching (age, time)
What time do you **get off** work, Stephen?	finish (work, school)
These damp, miserable days **get** me **down**	depress me
I tried to phone you last night, but I couldn't **get through**	get a connection
He'll call the police if you don't **get off** his land	leave (an area)
How did the burglars **get in**?	enter the premises
I might **get round to** writing the letter tonight	find the time or energy to do it
The train **gets in** at 7.33	arrives

● Give

He's **given up** smoking at last	stopped
When are you going to **give back** that book I lent you?	return
Please **give** your homework **in** tomorrow morning	submit/hand in
They're **giving away** free sardines at the supermarket	giving for free
Which flowers are **giving off** that strange scent?	emitting
Our fuel is **giving out**	being used up
The government eventually g**ave in** to their demands	agreed to accept

● Go

My alarm **goes off** at 7.00 every morning	rings (clock)/explodes (bomb)
The price of grapefruit has **gone up**	increased
The fire has **gone out**	been extinguished
Let's **go over** the song once more, Pauline	practise/rehearse
Why don't you **go on with** your story?	continue
I've **gone** right **off** peach melba ice-cream	stop liking
He's **going through** a difficult period at the moment	experiencing
I don't really want to **go into** your personal problems	discuss
The opera house has **gone up** in flames	caught fire
A man **went for** Bill with a knife, but he wasn't hurt	attacked
You really can't **go around** wearing odd socks	go into public areas

Common phrasal verbs (continued)

How shall I **go about** telling her the news?	approach/tackle
Do you think the council will **go ahead with** the new by-pass?	carry out their plan to build it
I think I'm **going down with** flu	beginning to suffer from
Do you think I should **go in for** the competition?	enter

● Hold

I couldn't **hold back** my laughter when he told me	control
The traffic was **held up** for two hours this morning	delayed
Can you **hold on** a moment?	wait
Three armed robbers **held up** a bank in Surrey today	robbed by force
I'll **hold on to** my beliefs until I die	maintain
The government can't **hold down** this nation for ever	oppress
The bridge is **held up** by three pairs of columns	supported
The army **held back from** taking the town	refrained from
You can **hold off** a cold by eating garlic	prevent

● Keep

Danger! **Keep out**	Do not enter
Do you think you can **keep up** this level of work?	maintain
I wish you wouldn't **keep on** whistling	continue/persist in
I couldn't **keep up with** the champion	run as fast as
I use this special candle to **keep** the mosquitoes **off**	prevent them settling on me
I think we'd better **keep off** that subject for the moment	avoid

● Look

Who's going to **look after** the children while I'm away?	take care of
Can you just **look through** these accounts for me?	check
Look out for spelling mistakes	check minutely
Look out! There's a cow behind you	pay attention
I've **looked up** his name in the phone book, but I can't find it	look for a citation or reference
Everyone **looks on** you as the leader	regards
I can't stay long – I'm just **looking in**	paying a short visit

● Make

I can't **make out** what it says on that notice	distinguish
Valerie and Chris have **made up** again	become friends
That stupid story was **made up** by the press	invented
You've **made** me **out** to be a monster	misrepresented
Their house is being **made over** for that stupid programme	renovated

● Pull

I'm going to have a tooth **pulled out**	extracted
They're going to **pull** the old school **down**	demolish
Do you think he will **pull off** the deal?	be successful with
We can **pull** the situation **round** if we all work together	improve/bring back to normal
Who has **pulled** all the petals **off** the roses?	removed
She's in a critical condition, but I think she will **pull through**	survive/recover
A sinister-looking purple car **pulled up** outside	stopping
Who **pulled up** the rhododendrons?	removed from the ground

● Put

Could you **put** me **through to** Mr. Parragueno?	connect (on the phone)
We'll have to **put off** our holiday	postpone
She **put over** her points very effectively	communicated
How long will it take to **put** the shed **up**?	build/construct
Put on your coat – we're going for a walk	wear/don
It took three days to **put out** the fire	extinguish

Common phrasal verbs (continued)

*Are you going to **put forward** your proposal?*	propose
*Could you **put** me **up** for the night?*	give me a bed

● Run

*Can we **run over** the instructions again?*	check
*He always **runs away from** difficult situations*	avoids
*The government have **run out of** ideas*	exhausted
*Her brakes failed and she **ran into** the car in front*	collided with
*A lot of hedgehogs get **run over** when crossing motorways*	hit by cars
*People are always **running** Mrs. Smythe **down***	criticising unfairly
*Lord Clop **ran** Lord Flop **through**, wounding him fatally*	pierced his body with a sword

● See

*Will you **see** me **off** at the airport?*	come and say goodbye
*Can you **see to** the guests? I need to get changed*	look after
*I **saw through** his lies straight away*	perceive falsity
*I've just got enough money to **see** me **through***	to help me survive
*Let's **see about** finding somewhere to stay*	start trying to find
*Say what you mean – I can't **see into** your devious mind*	read
*From the chalet you can **see out over** a beautiful lake*	have a view of

● Set

*She **set up** as a jeweller two years ago*	established a jeweller's business
*One spark was all it took to **set off** the explosion*	make it happen
*What time did they **set off**?*	leave/'depart
*Could you **set out** your ideas on paper?*	write down
*The rain looks as if it has **set in** for the day*	become established
*He **set out** to become the champion from an early age*	planned
*The company was **set up** by a convicted fraudster*	established/founded
*The goods were **set out** in ten rows*	arranged

● Take

*He **took up** tennis at the age of 43*	started (hobby, sport)
*His story **took** me **in** completely*	deceived me
*Do you think she **takes after** her mother?*	resembles (in looks or behaviour)
*Why don't you **take off** your coat if you're hot?*	remove
*You've **taken on** an awful lot of work*	assumed responsibility for
*She never really **took to** her job*	began to like
*She was completely **taken aback** by his rudeness*	shocked
*We'll have to **take** it **apart** to see how it works*	take it to pieces
*We have to stop them **taking over** our business*	assuming control of
*Can you **take** me **round** the city centre?*	show me
*I'm **taking over from** Mrs. Sphinx next week*	assuming her position
*Did you manage to **take down** all the information?*	write down

● Turn

*This factory **turns out** 33,000 sprockets every year*	produces
*I expect he'll **turn up** for dinner*	arrive
*My application has been **turned down***	rejected
*When I challenged him, he **turned on** me*	attacked (verbally or physically)
*Can you **turn on/turn off** the light?*	flick the light switch on or off
*Can you **turn** that music **down**, please?*	reduce the volume
*At midnight the frog **turned into** a minor royal personage*	was transformed into
*Can you stop **turning over**? I can't sleep*	revolving laterally (in bed)
*I'll pay you £10 to **take away** my old sofa*	remove

Verb + non-finite forms

-ing	He **admitted** breaking the vase • She **detests** watching soaps I **dread** having to meet him • We **miss** rowing on the lake I don't **recall** buying it • She **loathes** baking bread Have you quite **finished** mocking? • Try to **avoid** making mistakes I **suggest** lying on your side • She **celebrated** passing her exams Do you **fancy** having an ice-cream? • Don't **delay** claiming your refund The students **celebrated** passing the exam • I can't **stand** sitting in a draught
being done	He **resents** being shouted at • I **hate** being delayed I don't **remember** being hit • He **mentioned** being contacted You **risk** being arrested • The cat **adores** being stroked
having done	He **denied** having broken the vase • She **regrets** having met him They don't **remember** having bought it • Do you **recall** having eaten it?
to-infinitive	They **neglected** to water the delphiniums • I **voted** to abolish conscription Don't **fail** to contact me • **Prepare** to welcome the sub-vice-secretary He **claims** to have won a medal • I **fight** to win • We were **forced** to stand She has **vowed** to stand again • She **managed** to swim to safety The government **pledged** to cut waiting times • I didn't **choose** to stay here I don't **intend** to resign • She**'s longing** to go to Mandalay He **attempted** to stab a policeman • Jonah **survived** to live another day I didn't **consent** to appear in your newspaper • You will **learn** to obey She **pretended** to eat the pudding • We **paid** to have a better service than this
to be done	We **expect** to be informed • He **hopes** to be selected She **tends** to be teased • They **opted** to be sent to the northern sector
to have done	He **proved** to have stolen the goods • I **happen** to have met Sir Jonathan She **claims** to have climbed Ben Nevis • It **seems** to have broken
Object + *-ing* form	I **heard** them coming in • I can't **imagine** her failing We couldn't **prevent** the rock falling • The news **sent** us reeling They **found** him lying face down • Don't **keep** them waiting They **caught** him stealing • I **felt** a spider crawling up my leg She stopped the baby **falling** in the gravy • I can just **picture** him laughing
Object + *to* infinitive	They **forbade** us to touch the samples • I **challenge** you to throw it She **persuaded** me to go to the party • I **urge** you to see it Scott **inspired** him to write • They **trained** the chimp to use sign language She **encouraged** me to apply • They **obliged** us to wait She **taught** me to knit • The offer of filthy lucre **induced** him to break the law
Object + base form	The teacher **made** us wait • Don't **let** them eat the strawberries We **saw** him fall • I **felt** something hit me in the back of the neck
Object + Past Participle	He **had** his bike stolen • Why don't you **get** your leg examined? We **found** the cottage burnt • She **ordered** the goods sent back He **needs** his head tested • We **want** the money refunded
Preposition + *-ing*	I don't **object to** standing • Are you **afraid of** flying? She's **keen on** ski-ing • He's **gone off** hang-gliding I'm not **interested in** sub-letting • He was **saved from** drowning You've **put** me **off** jumping • I was **thinking of** going on a picnic She**'s against** going • I'm **looking forward to** retiring
for + object + *to* infinitive	We **arranged** for them to visit the museum • Don't **wait** for me to finish They **called** for the Prime Minister to resign • She **paid** for him to have lessons They **pleaded** for the hostages to be released • I **asked** for the dog to be fed We **voted** for taxes to be raised • They **opted** for their pensions to be frozen
Verb in passive + *to* infinitive	He **is said** to live in Spain • She **is known** to have travelled to Algeria They **are reported** to be massing on the border • You **are not required** to bow He **is rumoured** to have lost a fortune • She **is thought** to have left He **was deemed** to be offside • She **is reckoned** to be the smartest student

Verb groups followed by *-ing*

Anticipation	I can't **imagine** performing on stage I don't **anticipate** them/their turning down the invitation I might **envisage** eventually working in the public sector
Avoidance	I couldn't **avoid** hitting the bollard He **evaded** being detected for two weeks You can't **escape** doing the garden
Beginning	When did you **begin** collecting beetles? If it **starts** raining, we'll have to give up the whole project He **commenced** moaning almost as soon as we arrived at the flat
Contemplation	He's **contemplating** moving to Barbados Would you **consider** changing your mind?
Continuation	He **continued** walking along the river bank I wish you wouldn't **keep** whistling When are they going to **resume** dredging?
Disliking	He just **hates** sitting in front of the T.V. I quite **dislike** cycling in the rain She **detests** performing in public I **loathe** weeding and raking
Ending	We only **finished** painting the kitchen this morning You really ought to **stop** biting your nails They didn't **cease** squabbling all afternoon
Fear	He never **feared** meeting the most difficult obstacles I really **dread** going back on stage
Involvement	Being a policeman **means** tramping the streets at all hours Visiting Fred usually **involves** getting through a few glasses of wine Playing a musical instrument **entails** doing a lot of practice
Liking	She quite **likes** playing badminton I **love** messing about on boats The children **adore** going to the seaside We really **enjoyed** beating the carpets
Memory	Do you **remember** going boating last summer? I don't **recall** ever meeting him He says he doesn't **recollect** seeing anyone enter the building I'll never **forget** eating porridge with honey
Objection	I don't **mind** doing the washing up She **resents** being told what to do I **object to** being served cold potatoes
Permission (general)	We don't **allow** listening to music while working Do they **permit** taking pictures in here? We don't **tolerate** people heckling
Postponement	Don't **delay** sending in your application She **put off** making the decision for as long as possible We can't **postpone** having the meeting indefinitely
Prohibition (general)	The teacher **forbade** smooching in class The council are going to **prohibit** cycling through the park When did they **ban** smoking in public places?
Recommendation (general)	I wouldn't **advise** using a direct flash I **suggest** taking things one step at a time They **recommend** visiting Hermitage Park when you are in Moscow

Verb groups followed by *to* infinitive

Advice (+ person)	*We do **urge** all walkers to take extreme care* *What would you **advise** me to do in this situation?* *They **recommended** me to visit the Pushkin Gallery*
Appearance	*The rain **seems** to have eased* *They don't **appear** to be hurrying*
Arrangement	*Have you **arranged** to see a doctor yet?* *I'm **planning** to take a tour of the Hebrides*
Attempt	*I **tried** to warn her, but it was no good.* *He **attempted** to climb the mountain without ropes* *Could you **endeavour** to keep up with the workload?*
Begging (+ person)	*She **implored** me to come to her aid* *He **begged** her to consider his request*
Compulsion (+ person)	*She **forced** us to dig a long trench* *We were **obliged** to stand for the whole journey* *Circumstances **compel** us to decline the invitation* *They **require** you to send in three copies*
Entitlement	*Pensioners are **entitled** to travel free of charge* *He isn't **eligible** to vote yet*
Help (+ person)	*Will you **help** me (to) put up the decorations?* *Can I **assist** you to carry that extremely heavy package?*
Hesitation	*I would **hesitate** to make such a categorical statement* *He **paused** to take breath before continuing*
Intention	*I **hope** to find a new job soon* *She **intends** to spend a year in Brazil before going to university* *He **proposes** to set up a new rubber company*
Memory	*Did you **remember** to put the dustbins out?* *She **forgot** to turn off the gas*
Offer	*She **volunteered** to send out the invitations* *He has never **offered** to give me a lift*
Order (+ person)	*They **ordered** the bakers to cut thicker slices* *You are **commanded** to attend Her Majesty* *Don't **tell** me what to do* *The divers were **instructed** to go inside the wreck*
Permission (+ person)	*I might **allow** you to kiss my hand* *We weren't **permitted** to rest for one moment*
Persuasion (+ person)	*You'll never **persuade** him to change his mind* *Her arguments **convinced** me to drop the case* *I can't **get** him to talk at all* *A small present might **induce** him to accept our offer*
Promise	*The company **guarantees** to replace all faulty goods* *We do not **undertake** to provide food or drink for the journey* *She **promised** to be on time for the interview*
Request (+ person)	*He was **invited** to present a paper at the conference* *They **asked** her to join the Board of Directors* *You are **requested** to appear before the committee*
Stimulation (+ person)	*Their response **prompted** us to withdraw our offer* *Your moaning doesn't exactly **stimulate** me to make an effort*
Wanting	*She **yearns** to return to Indonesia* *I'm **longing** to see the fens again* *Do you **want** to come in for some coffee?*

Uses and Functions of Tenses

● Future simple: *will* + base form

Contingent future actions	If he doesn't come soon, **I'll leave**
Determination	I **will go** to China • We **shall stand up** for our rights
Insistence	You **will go** to bed • They **will do** their homework
Offer	**I'll do** the washing-up • **Shall I open** the window?
Prediction	He**'ll be** here soon • Rain **will spread** southwards
Promise	**I'll pay** you back tomorrow • We**'ll let** you know
Scheduled event	This shop **will re-open** on November 21st
Second of two future actions	**I'll feed** the ducks when I've mended the bike

● Future continuous: *will* + *be* + *-ing*

Assumption	You**'ll be coming** to the party, I suppose?
Expected events	The plane **will be landing** shortly
Progressive action around a punctual action	**I'll be sleeping** when you get back
Progressive action around a stated time	We**'ll be eating** at eight o'clock
Scheduled events	The procession **will be arriving** in five minutes
Surmise about a present action	They**'ll be lounging** on the beach by now

● Future perfect simple: *will* + *have* + past participle

Action completed before a stated time	We**'ll have painted** it all by this afternoon
Assumption	You**'ll have been paid for**, I assume
Surmise about a recent action	She**'ll have had** the operation by now

● Future perfect continuous: *will* + *have* + *been* + *-ing*

Assumption	You**'ll have been getting** organised, I expect
Defined duration up to a stated future time	**I'll have been working** here for 10 years by next June
Surmise about a recent action	He**'ll have been drinking** again

● Present simple: *I/you/we/they* + base form; *he/ she/it* + base form + *-s*

Commentary	Hoofer **passes** the ball to Slicer • ... and Murray **nets**
Expressing opinion	I **agree** entirely • I **don't doubt** what you say
Generalisations	Middle-aged men **tend** to have paunches
Habit	She **eats** organic food • I always **sprinkle** it with salt
Immutable facts	The earth **goes** round the sun • 7x73 **equals** 511
Instructions	You **mix** the flour and water, and then you **add** rosemary
Origins	Marzipan **comes** from Italy • Peasticks **are made** in Cumbria
Plot summary	Polonius **makes** a noise and Hamlet **stabs** him
Processes	The paper **is** then **separated** into batches
Routine	We **feed** the goldfish every morning
Schedule	We **visit** the pagoda at 10.00, then **have** coffee
State	He **knows** Diss well • They **own** several old masters
Timetable	The boat **leaves** at 6.40 • The concert **starts** at 5.00

● Present continuous: *I am, you/ we/they are* + *-ing*; *he/ she/ it is* + *-ing*

Action currently in progress	We**'re drinking** daiquiris right now
Arranged actions	We**'re lunching** with the Dicks tomorrow
Behaviour	You**'re being** rather obnoxious, Baldwin
Change of state	You**'re getting** fat • The milk**'s going** off
Regrettable habit	He**'s** always **putting** his clumsy foot in it
Temporary habits	He**'s jogging** a lot these days • I**'m working** mornings this week
Temporary states	I**'m working** in Glasgow this week
Trends	The planet **is heating** up • Share prices **are falling**

Uses and functions of tenses (continued)

● Present perfect simple: *I/ you/ we/ they have; he/she/it has* + past participle

Action within present time phase	She**'s lost** three jobs this year • I**'ve drunk** two teas today
Experiences, unstated time	I**'ve climbed** Ben Nevis • **Have** you ever **eaten** flamingo?
Long-term states, stated time period	We**'ve been** sober for two years • I**'ve lived** here since Easter
Permanent habits	He**'s** always **snored** • I**'ve smoked** all my life
Prior action, unstated time	I**'ve** already **peeled** them • She**'s** already **broken** it
Reason for present state	I can't come - I**'ve lost** my ticket • I'm gobsmacked – it**'s gone!**
Recent actions	They**'ve** just **bought** a tractor • I**'ve** recently **had** flu
Repeated action over a period of time	I**'ve collected** beer mats for years • I**'ve jogged** since 1972

● Present perfect continuous: *I/ you/ we/ they have; he/she/it has + been* + past participle

Reason for present state	I'm exhausted - I**'ve been working** all night
Recent activity	I**'ve** just **been clearing** out the attic • He**'s been dancing**
Regular or intermittent action	I**'ve been playing** tennis for years • She**'s been writing** since 1998
Short-term states	I**'ve been living** here for three months
Unbroken action	He**'s been whistling** for hours • You**'ve been sleeping** since 9.00

● Past simple: past form

Contemporaneous actions	Adam **vacuumed** while Eve **sorted out** the books
Creation, invention, unstated time	Faust **was written** by Goethe • Who **built** Luton?
Durative action, stated period	He **laughed** for half-an-hour • They **chatted** for ages
Durative action, unstated period	He **studied** at Lancaster • She **played** tennis for Nigeria
Historical fact, stated time	India **became** independent in 1947 • Alfred **reigned** from 871
Historical fact, unstated time	The Harappan civilization **grew up** in the Indus Valley
Hypothesis	If I **knew** what to do, I would do it
Narrative sequence (usually written)	The fox **crept** into the garden and **lay** down
Past habit	She **went** to school at 8.30 every day • He often **hummed**
Politeness	**Did** you **require** anything else, sir?
Punctual action, stated time	They **demolished** the hospital last year
Punctual action, unstated time	He **died** on a ship • She **played** in the Philharmonia
Reason for present state	She's crying because she **failed** • We **won!** I'm over the moon!
Repeated action, stated period	We **swam** all summer • The dog **barked** for ages

● Past continuous: *I/he/she/it was; you/we/they were* + *-ing*

Contemporaneous actions	Carol **was digging** while Jack **was mowing**
Intention	I **was thinking** of going to Germany
Progressive action around a punctual action	They **were cooking** when the phone rang
Progressive action around a stated time	I **was jogging** at 8.00 • She **was bathing** at 3.00 a.m.
Scene-setting in narrative	It **was snowing** when Dr Bates got to the manor
Tentativeness	I **was wondering** if you would like to come with us

● Past perfect simple: *had* + past participle

Abnormal order of actions	He went through the lights before they **had changed**
Action prior to stated action	When I got back, she **had changed** all the locks
Action prior to stated time	I **had answered** all the letters by 3.00
First of two past actions	He **had** just **lost** his job when I saw him
Reason for past state	She **had eaten** some bad fish and was feeling queasy
Scene-setting in narrative	I **had** just **been** on a long journey
Tentativeness	I **had thought** we might go to the Geology Museum
Unfulfilled condition	If they **had caught** a taxi, they would have won

● Past perfect continuous: *had + been + -ing*

Reason for past state	The room stank - someone **had been smoking**
Scene-setting in narrative	The boys **had been building** a tree house

Tenses with typical time expressions

Present Simple	I eat cornflakes **every day/on Sundays** She goes swimming **once a week/all the time** He **never/rarely/sometimes** watches television They **often/usually/always/frequently/seldom** eat fish with peas
Present Continuous	Prices are rising very quickly **at the moment/right now** I'm feeling slightly unwell **today** We're having dinner at 7.00 **tonight** She's meeting Bill **next Thursday/tomorrow**
Present Perfect Simple	I've been to Paris **three times/ø** I've written three letters **this morning/this week/ø** He's **just/already/recently** found a new job She hasn't done it **yet/so far** Have you **ever** seen the Queen?
Present Perfect Continuous	She's been smoking **for five years/for the last six months/since 1992** We've been travelling **recently/Ø** I've been playing tennis **again**
Past Simple	I went to London **last week/month/year** She graduated **four years ago/in 2001** He arrived **yesterday/at 8.00** He ran away **when he saw the spider**
Used to	He used to eat worms **when he was a child/ø** We used to have an open fire **in those days/ø**
Past Continuous	I was having dinner **at 8.00 last night** He was having a bath **when she arrived** They were chatting **throughout the lesson**
Past Perfect Simple	I had **just** got up **when the postman knocked** We had **already** eaten the pie **before they arrived** They had finished the trench **by the time I got there**
Past Perfect Continuous	I had been working hard **all morning/for five hours** She had been sleeping **when I came in**
Future Simple	I'll tell him **when I see him/next week** I'll see you **on Saturday/before too long** I'll take an umbrella **if it rains/in case it rains** He'll probably arrive **at about 10.00/soon**
Going to	I'm going to visit Japan **next spring/soon** We're going to see Father Christmas **this afternoon/later on**
Future Continuous	I'll be having my dinner **at 8.00/when you arrive** The plane will be landing **shortly**
Future Perfect Simple	I'll have finished **by 10.00/by the time he calls** They'll have arrived **by now**
Future Perfect Continuous	I'll have been working here for ten years **by next October** She'll have been sleeping **when we get there**

Syntactic classification of full verbs

- **Intransitive verbs: subject = agent**

Subject	Verb	Commonly used verbs
She	is sleeping	go, think, sit, smile, act, look,
The horse	has died	die, dance, decide, appear

- **Ergative verbs: subject = patient; agent unknown**

Subject	Verb	Commonly used verbs
The door	opened	close, fall, break, melt, break, fly,
The rice	is cooking	boil, ring, burn, spill, dry

- **Copular verbs: complement = definition/description of subject**

Subject	Verb	Complement	Commonly used verbs
Our house	is	quite warm	look, seem, appear, taste, smell,
She	has become	a bit of a pain	feel, become, go, turn, get

- **Affective verbs: subject = patient; direct object = affective agent**

Subject	Verb	Direct object	Commonly used verbs
We	loved	the broccoli	like, love, adore, enjoy, relish,
The dog	hates	old bones	hate, loathe, detest, abhor

- **Monotransitive verbs: subject = agent; obligatory direct object = patient**

Subject	Verb	Direct object	Commonly used verbs
You	broke	the vase	make, do, construct, destroy,
Our neighbour	makes	garden gnomes	hold, carry, expel, infect

- **Monotransitive verbs: optional omission of direct object**

Subject	Verb	Direct object	Commonly used verbs
She	has eaten	(her dinner)	cook, write, ride, drink, sing,
He	writes	(poetry/novels)	play, clean, wash, shoot

- **Reflexive verbs: subject = agent and patient**

Subject	Verb	Reflexive pronoun	Commonly used verbs
He	cut	himself	hurt, admire, inject, defend, kill,
The Kales	have insured	themselves	congratulate, cure, hate, punish

- **Reciprocal verbs: double/plural subject = agent and patient**

Subject	Verb	Reciprocal pronoun	Commonly used verbs
The team members	congratulated	one another	hurt, admire, love, defend,
The twins	admire	each other	congratulate, kiss, hate, see

- **Ditransitive verbs: indirect object (recipient) before direct object (patient: obligatory)**

Subject	Verb	Indirect object	Direct object	Commonly used verbs
Jill	owed	Jack	some money	send, pass, bring, take, write,
They	are giving	her	a camera	read, blow, tell, show

- **Ditransitive verbs: direct object (patient) before indirect object (recipient: optional)**

Subject	Verb	Direct object	Indirect object	Commonly used verbs
She	sent	some seahorses	(to her grandson)	send, pass, bring, take, write,
He	passed	the ball	(to the wing)	read, blow, tell, show

- **Complex transitive verbs: subject = agent; direct object = patient; complement**

Subject	Verb	Direct object	Complement	Commonly used verbs
He	rolled	the pastry	flat	knock, make, put, make, set,
I	hung	the picture	straight	lay, want, find, throw, squash

Passives

Verb form	Active voice	Passive voice
Present Simple	We **cut** the grass once a week They often **phone** me at night	The grass **is cut** once a week I **am** often **phoned** at night
Present Continuous	Someone**'s ringing** the bell A cow **is staring** at me	The bell **is being rung** I**'m being stared** at by a cow
Present Perfect Simple	They **have closed** the road Someone **has smashed** the tulips	The road **has been** closed The tulips **have been smashed**
Present Perfect Continuous	Someone **has been drinking** the wine We**'ve been painting** the fence	The wine **has been being drunk*** The fence **has been being painted***
Past Simple	The postman **bit** the dog We never **found** them	The dog **was bitten** by the postman They **were** never **found**
Used to	They **used to cook** it like this The teachers **used to hit** us	It **used to be cooked** like this We **used to be hit** by the teachers
Past Continuous	They **were mending** the gutters Someone **was playing** a violin	The gutters **were being mended** A violin **was being played**
Past Perfect Simple	Someone **had found** it in the grass They **had brought** it from Mexico	It **had been found** in the grass It **had been brought** from Mexico
Past Perfect Continuous	They **had been eating** the tulips We **had been washing** the spoons	The tulips **had been being eaten*** The spoons **had been being washed***
Future Simple	We **will contact** you No-one **will reveal** the secret	You **will be contacted** The secret **will not be revealed**
Future Continuous	They**'ll be demolishing** the hut Someone **will be making** the tea	The hut **will be being demolished*** The tea **will be being made***
Future Perfect Simple	They **will have built** it by April I**'ll have sent** it by tomorrow	It **will have been built** by April It **will have been sent** by tomorrow
Infinitive	I don't want them **to tell** me You ought **to have washed** it	I don't want **to be told** It ought **to have been washed**
-ing form	I don't like people **tickling** me I don't remember anyone **hitting** me	I don't like **being tickled** I don't remember **being hit**
-ing + past participle	I don't recall anyone **having phoned** me He's angry about June **having insulted**	I don't recall **having been phoned** He's angry about **having been insulted** by
Modals	You **can/could/should/must tell** him They **may/might/would have lost** it	He **can/could/should/must be told** It **may/might/would have been lost**
Marginal Modals	They **are going to sue** him You **have to fry** it	He **is going to be sued** It **has to be fried**

*These forms are unusual

• Agent, origin, instrument, material, recipient

Authorship: agent	*'Romeo and Juliet' was written **by Shakespeare**. • Guernica was painted **by Picasso***
Production: agent	*These biscuits are made **by Crumb & Co**. • This car was manufactured **by Ghost Inc**.*
Process: agent	*She was brought up **by her aunt**. • The rabbit was killed **by a fox**.*
Production: instrument	*These shoes were made **by hand**. • Steel is produced **by means of the puddling process**.*
Production: origin	*Grapes are grown **in Italy**. • Pencils are manufactured **in Sardinia***
Production: material	*Wine is made **from grapes**. • This flute is made **of silver**.*
Recipient	*The prize has been awarded **to Shelley Smith**. • The letter was handed **to your mother**.*

Conditional Forms

- **Zero conditional: always/in general: *If* + Present simple; Present simple**

> If dogs **eat** fish, they **get** sick • If there **are** any croissants, I usually **have** one or two
> If I **go** jogging in the mornings, I **feel** fit • If there **is** a good film on, we usually **go** and **see** it

- **First conditional: future/real: *If* + Present simple; Future simple**

> If I **find** your book, I'll **phone** you • **I'll move** the books if you **roll** the carpets up
> If you **touch** that switch, you'll get a shock • They **won't come** unless they **find** a baby-sitter

Alternative: *If* + *should* + base form; Future simple/base form

> If I **should find** them, I **will return** them to you • If it **should rain**, we **won't bother** with the picnic
> If you **should arrive** early, please **inform** us immediately • If there **should be** any problem, **call** us

Inversion: *Should* + Present simple; Future simple/base form

> **Should** we **miss** the train, we'll **catch** the bus • **Should** you **encounter** any snakes, **don't panic**
> **Should** you **mislay** this card, **contact** our advisers • **Should** I **find** any mistakes, you **will have** to do it again

- **Second conditional: hypothetical/unreal: *If* + Past simple; *would* + base form**

> If I **had** enough money, I **would buy** a new dress • If I **saw** any discrepancies, I **would correct** them
> If I **knew** where he **was**, I'd **get** in touch with him • If I **were** Prime Minister, I **would increase** taxation

Alternative: *If* + *could* + base form; *would/could* + base form

> If I **could swim**, I **would be** very happy • If we **could** just **find** out where he lives, we **could interview** him
> If they **could acquire** this land, they **would build** flats • If you **could have** a new car, what type **would** it **be**?

Alternative: *If* + *were* + infinitive; *would* + base form

> If it **were to rain**, we **would cancel** the garden party • If she **were to resign**, we **would vote** in a new leader
> If you **were to win**, what **would** you **do** with the money? • If sea-level **were to rise**, the coast **would disappear**

Inversion: *Were* + subject + infinitive; *would* + base form

> **Were** the tree **to fall**, it **would hit** the house • **Were** we **to be** evicted, we **would have** nowhere to go
> **Were** he **to have** an accident, he **would have** no cover • **Were** I **to fail**, I **would take** the exam again

- **Third conditional: past: *If* + Past perfect; *would/could/might* + *have* + Past participle**

> If I **had known**, I **would have told** you immediately • What **would** you **have done** if she **had fainted**?
> If he **hadn't drunk** so much, he **might have been** all right • They **could have crashed** if I **hadn't warned** them

Inversion: *Had* + subject + Past participle; *would/could/might* + *have* + Past participle

> **Had** the bomb **exploded**, it **would have caused** immense damage • **Had** I **fallen**, I **might have broken** my leg
> **Had** I **been** informed, I **would have** acted immediately • I **might have revealed** the truth **had** I **been** there

- **Mixed conditional: past to present: *If* + Past perfect; *would* + base form**

> If you **hadn't gone** to bed so late, you **wouldn't feel** so tired • If I **had woken up** in time, I **would go**
> If he **had caught** the bus, he **would be** here by now • If I **had stolen** it, my fingerprints **would be** on it

Other types of conditional clause

Sentence	Meaning
Unless you arrive soon, *you'll miss the soup course*	if you don't arrive soon
*You should recover **provided that you take this medicine***	if and only if you take the medicine
*We'll reinstate him **as long as he apologises***	if and only if he apologises
*I'll take some crab sandwiches **in case I get hungry***	because I might get hungry later on
*Take alternative route **in case of flooding***	if the road is flooded
*Make a note of it **lest you forget***	otherwise you might forget
***But for your help**, we wouldn't have got here in time*	if you hadn't helped us
*He'd be a good presenter **if it wasn't for his stutter***	if he didn't stutter
***Supposing the dog gets sick** – what will you do then?*	if the dog gets sick, by any chance
***All being well**, we should arrive by noon*	if nothing bad happens
***Other things being equal**, we should meet the deadline*	if other factors don't change
***Given that you have no experience**, we can't employ you*	if it's true that you have no experience
***Multiply 19 by 23 and** you get 437*	if you multiply 19 by 23
***Hand over the money or** I'll shoot you*	if you don't hand over the money
***If not for her heroism**, the crew might have perished*	if she hadn't been so heroic
*The picnic will go ahead, **weather permitting***	if the weather is good enough
*I'll sign the contract, **with the proviso that you omit clause 3***	only if you omit clause 3
***Even if he passes his exams**, he won't get the job*	it doesn't matter if he passes his exams
***Go to bed, otherwise** you'll get no porridge in the morning*	if you don't go to bed
*We might get a draw, **with a bit of luck***	if we are lucky
*Cook product for 25 minutes **if frozen***	if it is frozen
***Assuming that they accept**, where shall we take them?*	if we can assume that they will accept
*It won't taste very good **without salt***	if it doesn't have salt
***Only if you work hard will you** pass the exam*	if you don't work hard you won't pass
*We'll accept your offer **on condition that it is backdated***	only if it is backdated
***If you clean your room then** I'll consider it*	only after you have cleaned your room

Wishes

• Undesirable present state

Those lemons **are** really expensive	I wish they **weren't** so expensive
It**'s** raining	I wish it **wasn't** raining
I **haven't got** any money	I wish I **had** some money
I **don't know** where she **is**	I wish I **knew** where she **was**

• Regrettable past state

I **was** really angry	I wish I **hadn't been** so angry
They **weren't** very hospitable	I wish they **had been** more hospitable
I **didn't have** any money	I wish I **had had** some money
I **didn't know** he was coming	I wish I **had known** he was coming

• Undesirable present obligation

I**'ve got to** fill in my tax form	I wish I **didn't have to** fill in my tax form
We**'re obliged to** inform them	I wish we **weren't obliged to** inform them

• Regrettable past obligation

I **had to** send my passport	I wish I **hadn't had to** send my passport
We **were forced to** stand	I wish we **hadn't been forced to** stand

• Inability: present/future/general

I **can't** see the screen	I wish I **could/was able to** see the screen
I **can't** play the violin	I wish I **could** play the violin
She **can't** come tonight	I wish she **could** come tonight
It**'s not** possible to change it	I wish it **was/were** possible to change it

• Inability: past

I **couldn't** get a ticket	I wish I **had been able to** get a ticket
We **were unable to** find them	I wish we **could have found** them
I **couldn't** play	I wish I **could have played**
It **wasn't** possible to change it	I wish it **had been** possible to change it

• Undesirable habit

She **arrives** late every day	I wish she **didn't arrive** late every day
He **coughs** all the time	I wish he **didn't cough** all the time
He**'s** always **whistling**	I wish he **didn't/wouldn't whistle**
She never **stops fidgeting**	I wish she **would stop fidgeting**

• Desired action

The bus is late	I wish the bus **would come**
It's still raining	I wish it **would stop raining**
He's been unemployed for months	I wish he **would get** a job
They haven't repaired the lamp	I wish they **would repair** the lamp

• Regrettable past action/lack of action

She **shouted** at me	I wish she **hadn't shouted** at me
I **lost** my keys	I wish I **hadn't lost** my keys
I **didn't get** any onions	I wish I **had got** some onions
We **didn't send** them a card	I wish we **had sent** them a card

Reported Speech: Verb Changes

Present Simple **Past Simple**	*"I never **eat** cornflakes."* *He said he never **ate** cornflakes*
Present Continuous **Past Continuous**	*"I'm **having** trouble with my homework."* *She said she **was having** trouble with her homework.*
Present Perfect Simple **Past Perfect Simple**	*"They**'ve removed** the railings."* *He said they **had removed** the railings*
Present Perfect Continuous **Past Perfect Continuous**	*"We**'ve been eating** fish."* *They said they **had been eating** fish*
Past Simple **Past Perfect Simple**	*"I **bought** it yesterday."* *She said she **had bought** it the day before*
Past Continuous **Past Perfect Continuous**	*"The dog **was wagging** its tail"* *He said the dog **had been wagging** its tail.*
Past Perfect Simple **No change**	*"The streets **had emptied**"* *They reported that the streets **had emptied***
Past Perfect Continuous **No change**	*"They **had been digging**"* *He said they **had been digging***
Used to **No change**	*"We **used to play** soldiers"* *They said they **used to play** soldiers*
Going to *was/were going to*	*"We're **going to have** dinner"* *They said they **were going to have** dinner*
Future Simple *would do*	*"I**'ll open** the doors at 8.00"* *She said she **would open** the doors at 8.00*
Future Continuous *would be doing*	*"We**'ll be standing** by the window"* *They said they **would be standing** by the window*
Future Perfect Simple *would have done*	*"I**'ll have eaten** it by 10.30"* *She said she **would have eaten** it by 10.30*
Future Perfect Continuous *would have been doing*	*"She**'ll have been waiting** for us"* *He said she **would have been waiting** for us*
may *might*	*"We **may start** early"* *They said they **might start** early*
might **No change**	*"There **might be** some changes"* *They said there **might be** some changes*
can *could*	*"I **can let** you know tomorrow"* *She said she **could let** us know tomorrow*
could **No change**	*"I **could play** the oboe once"* *He said he **could play** the oboe once*
should **No change**	*"**You should try** this juice"* *She said we **should try** this juice*
would **No change**	*"**We would** never **let** you down"* *They said they **would** never **let** us down*
must (obligation) *had to*	*"I really **must go** to bed"* *He said he really **had to go** to bed*
must (deduction) **No change**	*"She **must be** away this weekend"* *He said she **must be** away this weekend*
have to *had to*	*"He **has to work** really hard"* *She said he **had to work** really hard*
ought to **No change**	*"You **ought to stop** complaining"* *She told us we **ought to stop** complaining*

Other Changes in Reported Speech

● Time: reporting a statement made in a different time-phase

*"I'm going to London **today**."*	*He said he was going to London **that day**.*
*"I bought this dress **yesterday**."*	*She said she had bought that dress **the previous day**.*
*"I'll tell him **tomorrow**."*	*She said she would tell him **the following day**.*
*"We're moving **this week/month/year**."*	*They said they were moving **that week/month/year**.*
*"I phoned him **last week/month**."*	*She said she had phoned him **the previous week/month**.*
*"I'm going to China **next month/year**."*	*He said he was going to China **the following month/year**.*
*"I saw them ten minutes **ago**."*	*She said she had seen them ten minutes **before/previously**.*
*"He resigned **the day before yesterday**."*	*She said he had resigned **two days previously**.*
*"She's coming **the day after tomorrow**."*	*He said she was coming **two days later**.*
*"They're asleep **now**."*	*She said they were asleep **then**.*
*"I'll send it **now**."*	*He said he would send it **immediately/straight away**.*
*"He's **currently** studying in Amsterdam."*	*She said he was studying in Amsterdam **at that time**.*
*"I'm busy **at the moment**."*	*She said she was busy **at that moment**.*

● Place: reporting a statement made in a different place

*"I'm staying **here**."*	*She said she was staying **there**.*
*"Do you like it **there**?"*	*She asked me if I liked it **here**.*
*"I can't stand **this place**."*	*He said he couldn't stand **that place**.*

● This, that, these, those: change of viewpoint

*"I love **this** cake."*	*She said she loved **that** cake.*
*"Where did you get **that** brooch?"*	*She asked me where I had got **this** brooch.*
*"**These** trees are lovely."*	*He said **those** trees were lovely.*
*"**Those** houses are ancient."*	*He said **these** houses were ancient.*

● Person: relationship to speaker

*"**You** are mad," he told me.*	*He told me **I** was mad.*
*"**You** can't come," he told her.*	*He told her **she** couldn't come.*
*"**I** don't feel well," she said.*	*She said **she** didn't feel well.*
*"**We** have finished," they said.*	*They said **they** had finished.*
*"She gave it to **me**," he said.*	*He said she had given it to **him**.*
*"This bag is **mine**," she said.*	*She said that bag was **hers**.*
*"We did it by **ourselves**," they said.*	*They said they had done it by **themselves**.*

Reporting verbs

● Verb + *to infinitive*

threaten, refuse, beg, prefer, agree, expect, swear, hope, claim	He **threatened to arrest** me • They **refused to go** to bed • She **begged to leave** He **prefers to eat** out • She **agreed to sell** me her car I **expect to hear** from you • I **swear to tell** the truth They **hope to go** to Mumbai • She **claimed to be** the Duchess of Cumberland

● Verb + person (object) + *to infinitive*

advise, warn, beg, remind, expect, persuade, recommend, ask, request, forbid, invite, urge, prefer, instruct	They **advised us to take** walking boots • She **warned me not to approach** He **begged his mother** to give him spinach • They **reminded us to set** the alarm We **expect you to write** every day • He tried to **persuade her to go** the cinema She **recommended me to visit** Jakarta • She **asked him to marry** her We **requested them to send** on our luggage • They **forbade us to chew** gum They **invited us to see** their garden • She **urged Chris to go** to the Swedish film She **prefers us not to shout** • He **instructed me to hold** the bow more loosely

● Verb + *-ing*

deny, admit, consider, suggest, propose, recommend, advise	He **denied eating** the trifle • She **admitted smashing** the vase Would you **consider selling** the house? • He **suggested buying** a new bicycle They **proposed going** by taxi • He **recommended trying** the venison She **advised reading** it in the original

● Verb + (*that*) + person (subject) + (*should*) + base form (optional *that* and *should*)

suggest, propose, demand, insist, recommend	She **suggested that I should eat** less chutney He **proposed that we take** some wine • They **demanded we open** our cases She **insisted we should return** the money • We **recommended they see** the tower

● Verb + person (object) + preposition + *-ing*

accuse, thank, congratulate, blame	She **accused me of eating** her grapes • I **thanked her for checking** the report They **congratulated us on winning** • He **blamed me for boiling** the artichokes

● Verb + (*that*) + person (subject) + finite verb form (*obligatory *that*)

say, boast, estimate, add, confirm, expect, point out, agree, mention, admit, report, observe, deny, state, hope, swear, reply, complain, claim, explain, disclose, confess	They **said** they were coming today • He **boasted that** he knew ten languages We **estimate that** we will arrive around 8.30 • He **added that** he had no money She **confirmed that** she would take the exam • She **expects that** you will accept *She **pointed out that** there was no bread • I **agree that** we have to economise *He **mentioned that** the tortoise had escaped • He **admitted** he had spilt the wine *He **reported that** the city was quiet • *She **observed that** the shelves were dusty He **denied** he had taken the keys • *She **stated that** the Queen had abdicated They **hoped** the beans would grow • He **swore that** he was not involved She **replied that** it was time to go • *We **complained that** the soup was cold She **claimed that** she had lost her bag • He **explained that** the shop was closed *She **disclosed that** she was divorced • He **confessed that** he had already eaten

● Verb + person (object) + (*that*) + person + finite verb form (*obligatory *that*)

tell, assure, remind, inform	She **told me that** she was late • I **assured him that** he could come in *He **reminded her that** the door was open *She **informed me that** the results were ready

● Verb + *if/whether/what/when/where/how/why/who* + finite verb form

ask, wonder, enquire, want to know, reveal, guess, know, remember	She **asked me where** the station was • They **enquired if** we had any vacancies He **wondered whether** she would come • She **wanted to know why** I was angry He wouldn't **reveal how** he had done it • I can't **guess why** she hit me Do you **know when** Lao Tze was born? • I can't **remember who** phoned

Types of Adverb

● Mode of action

Attitude	They **cheerfully** dismissed the allegations • I regard the matter very **seriously**
Intent	You kicked me **deliberately** • I **purposely** ignored his remarks
Manner	He runs **gracefully** • He started **hesitantly** • She cycles **carefully**
Quality	She sang **brilliantly** • They played **dreadfully**

● Time

Defined time	We planted the beans **yesterday** • I'll see you **later**
Duration	I won't stay **long** • It rained **briefly**
Frequency	They **often** go abroad • She **never** brushes her hair
Relation to present	The rabbit has **already** eaten • She hasn't got up **yet**
Sequence	**Firstly**, I'd like to say … • **Lastly**, could you put the eggcups in the dishwasher?

● Space

Direction	It's growing **inwards** • The demonstrators are coming **through**
Distance	The shops are quite **close** • The stadium is too **far** to cycle to
Position	Stick it **here** • Mrs. Greaves lives **opposite** • The pike is **downstairs**

● Extent

Amplification	I **thoroughly** disapprove of your action • He **bitterly** regretted leaving
Degree	I'm feeling **slightly** irritated • You run **quite** fast!
Diminution	I **almost** felt like walking out • I only **partly** believed her
Intensification	That's **absolutely** amazing! • She was **totally** in control
Scope	His works are **scarcely** known here • He is **widely** regarded as a genius

● Relative accuracy

Approximation	She's **about** twenty • It weighs **roughly** thirty kilos
Exactitude	They're hanging **exactly** level • That's **precisely** what I mean

● Speaker's attitude

Conviction	Mozart is **incontestably** the greatest composer • What you say is **patently** false
Emphasis	He **simply** never arrives on time • I was **literally** freezing
Focus	He eats **only** fruit • I was **especially** concerned to hear that she had resigned
Generalisation	**Overall**, they performed well • She is **generally** on time
Impression	**Interestingly**, he collects jugs • She was **strangely** listless
Judgement	He **foolishly** left the key in the lock • She **cunningly** delayed the pawn move
Style	**Frankly**, I think he deserves it • **Confidentially**, there's going to be a takeover

● Various

Command	**Here**, Rover! • **King's Cross**, please • **Out**!
Concession	He agreed. **However**, she didn't • They played well. **Nevertheless**, they lost
Discourse marker	**Now**, let's consider the finances • **Right**, I'll get the curling tongs
Doubt	Are you waiting to see me, **perhaps**? • She might **conceivably** have fainted
Probability	They're **probably** going to Cyprus • **Maybe** Raymond will be there
Respect	I'm in a bad way **financially** • They've gone up in the world **socially**
Result	I had to pay it all - **consequently**, I'm broke • I dropped it: **hence** it smashed
Specification	Two countries, **namely** England and France, have been chosen
Viewpoint	**Musically**, she is extremely talented • He is not her equal **intellectually**

Sentence-linking adverbials

Addition	His results are not very good. ***Furthermore***, he has no experience. His marriage is on the rocks. ***Moreover***, he's got a lot of debts. This bike's rather rusty. ***What's more,*** it's stolen. They're not as fit as their opponents. ***In addition***, they've got a man injured.
Amplification	I've never been to France. ***As a matter of fact***, I've never been to Europe. I'm not too fond of lettuce. ***To tell you the truth***, I can't stand it.
Automatic conclusion	I gave him your message. ***Of course***, he didn't say anything. She is a bit odd, though ***naturally*** I wouldn't say she was mad.
Clarification	It's a type of moth, actually. ***To be precise***, it's a cinnabar. She is a Piscean. ***That is to say***, her element is water. She lives in a small flat or, ***more accurately***, a bedsit.
Concession	She says she can't let me have the floral armchairs. ***Anyway***, I'm not interested. The rooms weren't up to much, but, ***at any rate***, we had a good time. We might as well unfurl the flag. ***In any event*** they can't arrest us for it.
Consequence	There are too many trees in the garden. ***For this reason*** we can't plant sunflowers. Bill lost his passport, and ***consequently*** we missed the flight back. Rats are carnivores, and carnivores eat meat. ***Therefore*** rats eat rabbits. Their cash flow situation deteriorated and ***hence*** they went bankrupt.
Contradiction	I don't support the government. ***On the contrary***, I'm one of its fiercest critics. We didn't cry over our defeat. ***Contrariwise***, we went and got blind drunk. People say Watt invented the steam engine. ***In actual fact*** he improved it.
Contrast	We don't normally employ school leavers. ***However***, we will consider your application. They fought hard, ***yet*** they lost the game I know it's a nice sofa. ***Nevertheless***, we can't afford to buy it. Her bow lost some of its hair in the last movement. ***In spite of this***, she kept going.
Enumerating reasons	I can't go this evening. ***In the first place***, I'm ill and ***secondly*** I haven't got any money. That house is quite unsuitable. ***For one thing***, it's got no bathroom.
Event change	You say we should go to the Rockies. ***Rather***, we ought to stay at home. She wanted to go to Darlington. ***Instead***, she ended up in Worcester.
Generalising	Contemporary British fiction has its high points, but ***generally*** it is somewhat patchy. He put in a few good tackles, and ***overall*** his performance was impressive. Dung beetles replenish the soil. ***In general***, they are good for the environment.
Qualifying	He complains rather a lot. ***At the same time***, he has his good points. It's a beautiful house. ***On the other hand***, it's rather out of the way.
Reformulating	She's Mexican, ***or rather***, she has a Mexican passport. He was being economical with the truth. ***In other words***, he was lying. It's a kind of lake. ***More precisely***, it's a periglacial lake.
Respect	I've got a cough and a sore throat. ***Otherwise*** I'm fine. She's a bit inexperienced. ***In other respects*** she's a very good candidate.
Similarity/ dissimilarity	Jill eats a lot of meat. Fred, ***likewise***, is a carnivore. We really must attack but, ***equally***, we mustn't lay ourselves open. He likes staying at home and watching T.V. ***Conversely***, she's very outgoing.
Specifying	I don't like shopping. ***In particular***, I don't like shopping for clothes. We want someone who knows foreign languages. ***Specifically***, we need a Greek speaker.
Strategic change of subject	I'm going to Stoke this afternoon. ***Incidentally***, the Wessons are coming to lunch. I do like your new sash windows. ***By the way***, can you lend me ten pounds?
Summing up	The food was good and the hotel was comfortable. ***All in all***, we had a good time. Unemployment is rising, businesses are folding. ***Altogether***, the economy is in a mess. Exploitation, chicanery, slaughter. ***To sum up***, the British Empire was a disaster.

Prepositions: main uses

Addition	*as well as* her cousins • *in addition to* his experience
Agent	*by* Goethe • *by* the police • *by* the thieves
Cause or reason	*because of* the hail • *on account of* his irritability • *out of* spite
Comparison	as big *as* a banana • stranger *than* fiction
Concession	*despite* his spots • *in spite of* their wealth • *notwithstanding* her arguments
Contrast	*in contrast to* chimps • *as distinct from* buttercups
Difference	different *from* his brother • distinct *from* this idea
Division	divided *by* religion • separated *from* their neighbours
Exception	*apart from* the expense • *except for* the youngest • *but for* his action
Instrument	*with* a rubber truncheon • *by means of* pulleys
Movement (area/surface)	*across* the Channel • *over* the carpet • *round* England • *off* the table
Movement (direction)	*towards* London • *away from* the fire • *in the direction of* the goal
Movement (line)	*along* the street • *across* the goal-line • *up* the road
Movement (passing)	*over* the trees • *round* the house • *past* the post office
Movement (point)	*to* London • *from* the station • (arrive) *at* the hotel
Movement (volume)	*into* the box • *through* the tunnel • *out of* the fridge
Origin	*from* China • *out of* the house • *from* the bowels of the earth
Position (adjacency)	*next to* the bank • *adjacent to* the boundary wall • *by* the river
Position (area)	*on* the premises • *within* the boundary • *off* the field
Position (distance)	*near* Luton • *far from* the farm • *as far as* London
Position (encirclement)	*surrounding* the building • *around* the pond • *surrounded by* a moat
Position (non-touching)	*behind* the sofa • *above* the clock • *beside* the river • *between* the bushes
Position (opposition)	*opposite* the bookshop • *facing* the park
Position (orientation)	*at the start of* the film • *at the end of* the street • *in the middle of* June
Position (parallel)	*parallel to* the railway line • *alongside* the liner
Position (section)	*at the front of* the hotel • *at the back of* the bus
Position (touching)	*on top of* the cupboard • *underneath* a pile of books • *against* the wall
Position (volume)	*inside* the cupboard • *outside* the garage • *in* the inner sanctum
Possession	the Houses *of* Parliament • the hind leg *of* a donkey
Purpose	*for* the money • *for* my own reasons
Respect	*with regard to* his promotion • *respecting* your application
Result	*as a result of* her carelessness • *as a consequence of* their policies
Similarity	*like* her mother • *similar to* that colour
Time (duration)	*for* eight hours • *during* the 19th century • *in* two days • *over* the weekend
Time (occasion)	*after* the film • *before* the lecture • *during* the meal
Time (reference point)	*on* Sunday • *by* 3.00 • *in* 1989 • *since* January 14th • *at* Christmas

Prepositions and adverbs of time

Approximate time/day/year	*around/about 9.00/midday/the 14th/1900*
At a point of time in the future	*in two days' time/five years' time*
At a point of time in the past	*two hours/three days/15 years **ago***
Before/after point of time/occasion	***before/after** Tuesday/11.00/the 23rd/Christmas/the film*
Between two times	***between** January **and** April • **from** 2003 **to** 2007*
Clock time	***at** 3.30/midnight/noon • twenty **to** nine • quarter **past** six*
Day in the past or future	***on** Friday/the 5th/Sunday morning/Christmas Day*
Duration of action/state	***for** ten minutes/four days/ 50 years/a long time/ages*
Festival/special occasion	***at** Christmas/Easter/New Year/the Winter Solstice*
From a point of time in the past	***since** 10.30/January 10th/2003/last Tuesday/I was a child*
Imprecise period	***in** my lifetime/modern times/the last few years*
Just after clock time	*(It's) **just after/just gone** 3.15/twenty past eight*
Just before clock time	*(It's) **nearly/almost** 10.00/6.30/midnight/closing time*
Last period	***last** week/month/year • **yesterday** • **yesterday** morning*
Latest time for completed action	***by** 11.30/next July/yesterday morning/2050*
Maximum period for completion	***within/over** the next two days/the last few hours*
Next period	***next** week/month/year • **tomorrow** • **tomorrow** afternoon*
Part of day	***in** the morning/the afternoon/the evening/the early hours*
Period before/after	*five minutes/three days/70 years **previously/before/later/after that***
This period	***this** week/morning/year/winter • **to**day/**to**night*
Time of cessation	***until/up to** 9.00/January 15th/the end of the week*
Time taken to do something	***in** 30 minutes/five years/a week/a split second*
Within a specified period	***during** their honeymoon/the film/the morning/the 16th century*
Year/decade/century/millennium	***in** 1568/the 1920s/the 18th century/the last millennium*

Verb + preposition + -ing/noun

• to

We **look forward to** meeting you • I **am not accustomed to** being spoken to like that

She **has taken to** drinking vodka at bedtime • The politician **confessed to** telling a small lie

I really **object to** receiving unsolicited mail • When are you going to **get down to** doing some work?

I'm **not up to** walking all the way there • He **is resigned to** losing his teeth

• of

He **was accused of** stealing the jewels • You should **take the opportunity of** seeing "The Flying Dutchman"

I often **dream of** sailing to distant countries • They **are afraid of** flying

He **is** not even **capable of** boiling an egg • She **has no intention of** marrying him

He **was found guilty of** riding on the pavement • She **was acquitted of** poisoning her husband

They **disapprove of** people wearing pink trousers • I **am** not particularly **fond of** snails

He **is ashamed of** his behaviour • They **suspect him of** telling lies

• on

He **counted on** winning first prize • You should **concentrate on** improving your goal kicks

She **insisted on** going to the most expensive restaurants • Don't **bank on** getting the last train

He's very **keen on** riding • He **prides himself on** his way of dressing

They **spend** a lot of **money on** horse-racing • I wouldn't **bet on him** coming before 10.00

• with

I wouldn't **entrust him with** repairing the pipes • He **was charged with** parking on a flowerbed

I'm **fed up with** hearing about your false teeth • He won't **be satisfied with** merely seeing it

She doesn't **agree with** using pesticides • We **alternate** cycling **with** weightlifting in our daily training

She **is** not **content with** merely being a secretary • I can't **cope with you** shouting at me all the time

Let's **experiment with** putting some garlic in it • I got **bored with** washing dishes

• in

He is totally absorbed **in** cleaning the carpet • She doesn't **believe in** making a fuss about nothing

He **takes pride in** keeping the fishtank clean • They **specialise in** repairing clockwork mice

She **succeeded in** jumping over the fence • There **is no point in** shouting at the traffic

He **is** very **interested in** collecting stamps • He doesn't often **indulge in** gardening

She **had no hesitation in** accepting the award • He sometimes engages **in** teasing people

• for

I'm not **in the mood for** roller skating • He **admired her for** winning the prize

I **apologise for** missing the appointment • He **was praised for** keeping his head in a crisis

The critics **condemned him for** taking liberties with the score • They **punished him for** stealing apples

What's your **excuse for** missing the lecture? • She's **responsible for** maintaining the boilers

• from

We get a lot of **benefit from** living in the countryside • I tried to **discourage him from** buying another TV

I **abstain from** eating chocolates on Sundays • I **get no pleasure from** telling you this

Teenagers **were banned from** entering • She's **suffering from** toothache

Illness **prevents him from** attending • The lifeguard **saved her from** drowning

Noun phrases

Pre-modifiers		Head	Post-modifiers	
Determiner(s)/ Quantifier(s)	Adjective/noun/ preposition	Noun/Pronoun/Ø	Prepositional Phrase	Relative/ non-finite clause
the		**man**	with brown shoes	
some of our	best	**students**		
this		**idiot**		who thinks he knows it all
	silly	**me!**		
a		**town**	in the Midlands	where we once stayed
my	old	**mate**	from university	
what an	awful	**mess**		
		cheese		made in Brittany
the	bus	**station**	in the centre	
a	measuring	**cup**		that I got in a jumble sale
six kilos of	choice	**tomatoes**	on the vine	
hardly any		**jam**		
		no-one	in the village	who I know
the	quickest	**Ø**	of us all	
this	precious	**stone**		set in the silver sea
the		**man**	in the moon	
all the three	plump	**pigeons**	on the bough	that were singing merrily
each		**slice**	of cake	
		she		who sits in state
the	up	**stroke**		
a piece of	blue	**paper**	on the photocopier	
which		**cats?**		
two	bald	**men**		eating cress sandwiches
a	cow's	**stomach**		

Prepositional phrases

• as

I go to bed at 11.30 **as a rule**	I'm a Virgo, **as a matter of fact**

• at

I'd say he's 50, **at a guess**	The kids are **at a loose end**
I'm completely **at a loss** to understand his behaviour	We must win **at all costs**
She spoke **at great length** about the regulations	She's a really kind person **at heart**
The escaped puma is still **at large**	Here we are **at last**!
It weighs **at least** two tons	I'll send it off **at once**
They chose the volunteers **at random**	There is a lot **at stake** in this election
The hero dies **at the end of** the film	We are **at war** with an implacable enemy

• behind

This city is **behind the times**	She's been very busy **behind the scenes**

• between

Between ourselves, I'm getting divorced	Reading **between the lines**, I can see he's unhappy

• by

You can borrow it **by all means**	I found the seal **by chance**
These toys are made **by hand**	I'm going to learn the regulations **by heart**
I called her number **by mistake**	I know her **by name**
This bus stops **by request**	I don't know him **by sight**
By the way, are you going to the party?	She broke it **by accident**
They've had a bust-up, **by all accounts**	He's a roofer **by profession**
She's very generous **by nature**	You took me quite **by surprise**
He's not royal **by birth**	They took the city **by force**

• for

They have split up **for good**	Will you do it **for her sake**?
Small pedal boats are **for hire** every afternoon	She won't do it **for nothing**
The sun's shining **for once**	He's called Bill **for short**

• from

I'm learning Tagalog **from scratch**	He gave his speech **from memory**

• in

I think we are basically **in agreement**	I thought her remark was **in bad taste**
Who's **in charge** here?	Who's **in command** of this brigade?
The two sisters have nothing **in common**	She told me about her childhood **in confidence**
The pool is 2.6 metres **in depth**	Is everybody **in favour**?
The car went up **in flames** on the first bend	The elderberries are **in flower**
Every part of the picture is **in focus**	The party was **in full swing** when Xi Yun arrived
Don't worry – you'll be **in good hands** with Rita	She is 1.65 metres **in height**
We drank a toast **in his honour**	I'm **in love** with these nodding dogs
You're **in luck** – they're serving shepherd's pie	The nation is **in mourning** for the great entertainer
We finished off the trifle **in no time**	He put his affairs **in order** before disappearing
I don't need any pills. I'm not **in pain**	The Queen is to visit us **in person**
It's not such a good idea **in practice**	I agree with the idea **in principle**
I've helped you. What will you do **in return**?	She kicked his shins **in revenge**
Artichokes are **in season**	She acted **in self-defence**
In short, we lost the game.	She's nowhere **in sight**. I don't think she's coming.
The phone is useful **in some respects**	Have you got any two-inch screws **in stock**?
What have you got **in store** for us, Mr. Punch?	I'm **in the dark** as to her intentions
Everything will be all right **in the end**	Share prices will go up **in the long run**
I'm not **in the mood** for playing tennis	The royal family is **in the news** again
He wants his name **in the newspapers**	Do you like gardening **in the nude**?
You always think you're **in the right**	We are all in the **in the same boat** – and it's sinking
An owl hooted **in the small hours**	It might work **in theory**, but not in practice
We didn't get there **in time**	We keep **in touch** by e-mail
Your instrument is not **in tune**	I'm **in two minds** about buying that tie
He looks quite good **in uniform**	The photocopier is currently **in use**
I searched for the drawing-pin **in vain**	He declared his love **in verse**, the soppy fool
This lump of gold is 4.3 kilos **in weight**	The table is 1.4 metres **in width**
Please inform us **in writing**	Please pay 50% **in advance**

Prepositional phrases (continued)

• *of*

These old boxes are **of no use**	This manuscript is **of no interest** to us
She is a woman **of principle**	The suspect is **of medium height**
He wants to be a man **of means**	John Blank, **of no fixed abode**

• *off*

You can drink when you're **off duty**	The goalkeeper is completely **off form**
She is completely **off her head**	You seem to be **off your food** today, Mildred

• *on*

He's gone **on a diet**	The fraudster is out **on bail**
I'm just here **on a visit**	He's going to Singapore **on business**
What time do you go **on duty**?	I'm feeling **on edge** – I can't concentrate at all
This Cambridge team is really **on fire**	You can't get there **on foot**
The centre forward is **on** terrific **form**	He is not **on good terms** with his cousin
He's got something **on his mind**	She's gone **on holiday** to Tenerife
My cello is out **on loan** at the moment	Can you apologise **on my behalf**?
Your books are **on order**	I don't eat veal **on principle**
The building is **on schedule**	I don't think I'll come, **on second thoughts**
Her work is **on show** at the Smooth Gallery	She's **on the night shift** at the moment
I applied for the job **on spec**	The railway workers are **on strike**
What's **on television** tonight? Same old rubbish?	New measures are **on the agenda**
He's got weddings **on the brain**	There's news **on the hour** every hour
This round of drinks is **on the house**	Fat-headedness is **on the increase**
I heard about the match **on the radio**	Their marriage is **on the rocks**
Pratap Patil is our reporter **on the spot**	If you're not **on time** you can't come in
He went **on trial** for murder	There are plenty of new paintings **on view**

• *out of*

My wife's **out of a job** at the moment	Slow down! I'm **out of breath**
These maps are **out of date**	The former health minister is **out of favour**
That photo of Elena is badly **out of focus**	He's **out of his depth** in this class
That cactus looks **out of place**	It went **out of print** after the first edition
Blackberries are just **out of season**	The rocket was **out of sight** within two seconds
Jelly babies are **out of stock**, I'm afraid	The news came **out of the blue**
Selling the house is **out of the question**	The Prime Minister is sadly **out of touch**
He sings completely **out of tune**	This lift is **out of use**

• *over*

Losing his job drove him **over the edge**	I'm **over the moon** – I've won £15 in the lottery
She was driving **over the limit**	The differential calculus went **over her head**

• *to*

She isn't planning to come, **to my knowledge**	The government is holding the workers **to ransom**
This novel is a bit over-written, **to my mind**	He controlled the ball **to perfection**
You whistling drives me **to distraction**	I don't drink **to excess**
Nobody can explain his disappearance **to this day**	We enjoyed ourselves **to the full**, didn't we Stella?

• *under*

The measures are currently **under discussion**	You must be **under a misapprehension**
She swore **under her breath**	These luxury apartments are **under offer**
The bridge is **under repair**	He is **under suspicion** for murder
I'm feeling somewhat **under the weather** today	The race is now **under way**

• *with*

The students responded **with enthusiasm**	She paid back his rudeness **with interest**
She welcomed me **with open arms**	It is **with great regret** that we must decline
£100 a week is just **within my budget**	The airport is **within earshot**, you'll be glad to know
The property is **within easy reach** of Szeged	Victory is **within our grasp**, girls
We tried unscrewing it, but **without success**	Everything went **without a hitch**
You must water the plants **without fail**	The lizards attacked **without warning**

Verb phrases

	Active	**Passive**
● **Base form**	*see*	*seen*
Negative	*not see*	*not seen*
Question	-----	-----
● **Infinitive**	*(to) see*	*(to) be seen*
Negative	*not (to) see*	*not (to) be seen*
Question	-----	-----
● **Present simple**	*see/sees*	*am/is/are seen*
Negative	*don't/doesn't see*	*am/is/are not seen*
Question	*do/does X see?*	*am/is/are X seen?*
● **Past simple**	*saw*	*was/were seen*
Negative	*didn't see*	*wasn't/weren't seen*
Question	*did X see?*	*was/were X seen?*
● **Future simple**	*will see*	*will be seen*
Negative	*won't see*	*won't be seen*
Question	*will X see?*	*will X be seen?*
● **Perfect infinitive**	*(to) have seen*	*(to) have been seen*
Negative	*not (to) have seen*	*not (to) have been seen*
Question	-----	-----
● **Present perfect simple**	*have/has seen*	*have/has been seen*
Negative	*have/has not seen*	*have/has not been seen*
Question	*have/has X seen?*	*have/has X been seen?*
● **Past perfect simple**	*had seen*	*had been seen*
Negative	*had not seen*	*had not been seen*
Question	*had X seen?*	*had X been seen?*
● **Future perfect simple**	*will have seen*	*will have been seen*
Negative	*will not have seen*	*will not have been seen*
Question	*will X have seen?*	*will X have been seen?*
● ***-ing* form/gerund**	*seeing*	*being seen*
Negative	*not seeing*	*not being seen*
Question	-----	-----
● **Continuous infinitive**	*(to) be seeing*	*(to) be being seen*
Negative	*not (to) be seeing*	*not (to) be being seen*
Question	-----	-----
● **Present continuous**	*am/is/are seeing*	*am/is/are being seen*
Negative	*am/is/are not seeing*	*am/is/are not being seen*
Question	*am/is/are X seeing?*	*am/is/are X being seen?*
● **Past continuous**	*was/were seeing*	*was/were being seen*
Negative	*was/were not seeing*	*was/were not being seen*
Question	*was/were X seeing?*	*was/were X being seen?*
● **Future continuous**	*will be seeing*	*will have been being seen*
Negative	*will not be seeing*	*will not have been being seen*
Question	*will X be seeing?*	*will X have been being seen?*
● **Perfect continuous infinitive**	*(to) have been seeing*	*(to) have been being seen*
Negative	*not (to) have been seeing*	*not (to) have been being seen*
Question	-----	-----
● **Present perfect continuous**	*have/has been seeing*	*have/has been being seen*
Negative	*have/has not been seeing*	*have/has not been being seen*
Question	*have/has X been seeing?*	*have/has X been being seen?*
● **Past perfect continuous**	*had been seeing*	*had been being seen*
Negative	*had not been seeing*	*had not been being seen*
Question	*had X been seeing?*	*had X been being seen?*
● **Future perfect continuous**	*will have been seeing*	*will have been being seen*
Negative	*will not have been seeing*	*will not have been being seen*
Question	*will X have been seeing?*	*will X have been being seen?*

Clause Structures

Subject	Verb
We	laughed
The old man	was drinking
Ancient cheese	stinks

Subject	Verb	Direct object
He	's watching	television
A spider	has bitten	me
Ø	Don't kick	the chair legs

Subject	Verb	Complement
Your hair	looks	nice
It	's getting	dark
Shakespeare	was	a playwright

Subject	Verb	Adverbial
The fridge	is	over there
They	argue	rather loudly
Our team	plays	on Sundays

Subject	Adverbial	Verb
I	sometimes	oversleep
She	hardly ever	complains
He	completely	froze

Subject	Verb	Direct object	Indirect object
I	gave	the oranges	to Tracy
We	are sending	some jam	to charity
The company	didn't deliver	the goods	to us

Subject	Verb	Indirect object	Direct object
She	won't give	me	the scissors
I	'll show	him	the ropes
My lawyer	has brought	me	the papers

Subject	Verb	Direct object	Complement
We	ought to paint	the bathroom	blue
They	want	him	alive or dead
You	could make	it	softer

Subject	Verb	Direct object	Adverbial
He	stuck	the notice	on the wall
She	plays	the clarinet	pretty well
The cat	has brought	a bird	into the house

Subject	Verb	Adverbial	Adverbial
She	arrived	at the airport	at 7.15
He	ran	upstairs	in a great hurry
The proofer	went	through this text	quite thoroughly

Adverbial Clauses

Type	Conjunctions	
Comment	as you know, all things considered, to be honest, I suppose, I reckon	**As you know**, we are unable to see any visitors I'm feeling pretty shattered, **to be honest** She's going to win the prize, **I reckon**
Comparison	as though, as, as if, like, just as	You talk **as if you were an expert on the subject** It seems **as though we'll have to wait** You don't want to get conned **like Brian did**
Concession	although, despite, in spite of, though, whereas, while, even if	**Although there was little food**, she survived **While I sympathise**, I think you could have tried harder It's a bad film, **even if it is well acted**
Condition	if, unless, provided that, as long as	I'll lend it to you **if you babysit for me** I'm going to leave **unless she gets here soon** I'm happy **as long as you're happy**
Exception	except (that), but that, save that, apart from (the fact that)	I'd treat you to lunch, **except that I haven't got any money** He would have passed the exam **but that he fell asleep** You'd think the parrot was dead, **save that it sometimes winks**
Excess	so ... that such ... that	She snores **so** loudly **that she often wakes the neighbours** He fried it at **such** a high temperature **that it burnt** They reacted **so** badly **that I decided not to mention it again**
Non-condition	whether ... or	**Whether you like it or not**, we're having broccoli **Whether or not it's Thursday**, I won't put the bins out **Whether you're young or old**, you'll enjoy the show
Place	where, everywhere, wherever	**Everywhere I go**, I get trouble I'm going **where no-one can find me** I wish you luck **wherever you end up**
Preference	rather than, sooner than	**Rather than go shopping**, I'd spend longer on the beach I'll resign **sooner than accept their terms** I'd die **rather than listen to his awful songs**
Proportion	As ... (so), the more ... the more the less ... the less	**As** he got hungrier, **(so) he grew angrier** **The more** I think about it, **the less I understand it** **The less** she eats, **the worse she looks**
Purpose	so that, in order to, to, so as to	I stole the money **so that you could buy the cat you want** I went to the butcher's **(in order) to buy some meat** They cut back the bushes **so as to allow freer access**
Reason	because, as, since, in case	I bit him **because he kicked me** **Since/As it was foggy**, I decided to stay in We'd better wait **in case he turns up**
Result	so that, so, with the result that	He went out with Jake, **so inevitably he got drunk** She ate a lot of sweets, **so that she became ill** I stubbed my toe, **with the result that the nail went black**
Simultaneity	no sooner ... than, hardly ... when/before scarcely ... when/before	I had **no sooner** got in **than the phone rang** She had **hardly** left school **when she became famous** We were **scarcely** indoors **before it began to hail**
Time	when, while, after, before, since, until, as	They stayed in the pub **until the barman kicked them out** Didn't you see her **when she came down to dinner?** A wasp came in **as I was shaving**
Unlimited scope	whatever, wherever, however, whoever, no matter	**Whatever prejudices you have**, keep them to yourself **Whoever her friend is**, he's got a really strange voice **No matter what I do**, I can never get the hang of it

Nominal Clauses

● *that* clauses

Subject	*That she can dance well* is beyond dispute
Direct object	I realised *that the kettle was boiling*
Subject complement	My feeling is *that interest rates will rise soon*
Appositive	His new theory, *that rhinos have a sense of humour*, is fascinating

● Subordinate *wh-* interrogative clauses

Subject	*What he earns* is nothing to do with me
Direct object	I'd like to know *how you plan to pay it back*
Prepositional complement	We can't agree on *where to put the hat rack*
Appositive	Your query, *how the grant was spent*, is dealt with under point 2

● *if* clauses

Direct object	Do you know *if there are any mangoes in the fridge*?

● *whether* clauses

Subject	*Whether he stays or goes* is nothing to do with me
Direct object	She can't decide *whether to give him the push or not*
Prepositional complement	It all depends on *whether the bath's been installed*
Appositive	Her speculation, *whether the company will fold*, might be well-founded

● *to* infinitive clauses

Subject	*To believe that* is the height of stupidity
Direct object	I forgot *to feed the fish*
Subject complement	The most sensible idea is *to go back to where we started*
Appositive	Their suggestion, *to re-lay the floor*, is unacceptable

● *-ing* clauses

Subject	*Feeling sorry for yourself* isn't going to help
Direct object	I loathe *defrosting the fridge*
Subject complement	Her hobby is *cultivating mushrooms*
Appositive	Her main responsibility, *organising the timetable*, is quite demanding

● Exclamative clauses

Displaced subject	It's extraordinary *how much he eats*
Direct object	I know *what a good athlete he is*

● Nominal relative clauses

Subject	*Whoever built that* was a genius (= *The person who built that* is a genius)
Direct object	He eats *what you give him* (= He eats *the food (that) you give him*)
Subject complement	That's *when I heard it* (= That's *the time (when) I heard it*)
Object complement	I put it *where he couldn't find it* (I put it *in a place where he couldn't find it*)

Relative clauses

● Restrictive/defining relative clauses with relative pronouns

Personal: subject	A driver **who crashed into a grocery** has been remanded in custody
Personal: object	The woman **who/whom/that/ø I saw** didn't look a bit like Tessa
Non-personal: subject	The egg **which/that cracked** had a reddish shell
Non-personal: object	The house **which/that/ø we want** is near the green belt
Preposition + object	The man **from whom we bought the chickens** is a local farmer

● Restrictive/defining relative clauses with relative determiners + noun

Personal: subject	A woman **whose dog attacked a jogger** has been fined £200
Personal: object	The doctor **whose treatment you so admire** has left the district
Non-personal: subject	The country **whose exports have increased the most** is China
Non-personal: object	The author **whose books you recommend** is giving a reading tonight
Preposition + object	The person **in whose house we are staying** is a famous writer

● Restrictive/defining relative clauses with relative adverbs

Time	The days **when children could freely play in the streets** are long gone
Place	Edinburgh is the city **where we got married**
Reason	That's the reason **why/ø he resigned**
Process	They had an arrangement **whereby Joe saw the children every weekend**

● Non-restrictive relative clause with relative pronouns

Personal: subject	The local M.P., **who believes in raising taxes**, is very unpopular
Personal: object	Mrs. Greaves, **(who)/whom you met at the party**, has died
Non-personal: subject	This machine, **which costs £3000**, is the latest model
Non-personal: object	Our house, **which we bought five years ago**, has barely appreciated
Preposition + object	These shears, **with which you are going to cut the hedge**, are the neighbour's

● Non-restrictive relative clause with relative determiners

Personal: subject	Alexei, **whose sister is a singer**, has decided to become a chef
Personal: object	Wellington, **whose portrait Goya painted**, was an irascible man
Non-personal: subject	Mexico, **whose biggest export is oil**, has a fast-growing economy
Non-personal: object	She told me I was mad, **which remark I decided to ignore**
Preposition + object	She arrived at 8.00, **by which time we had already left**

● Non-restrictive relative clause with relative adverbs

Time	I got my first spots in 1963, **when the Beatles were already famous**
Place	She was born in York, **where Auntie Joan used to live**
Process	He invested everything on the stock exchange, **whereby he was ruined**

© Peter Bendall 2010

Complementation

● Subject complements: copular verbs

Adjective	She seems **really nice** • He's getting **a bit cocky** • It's growing **late** That dress looks **too short** • That perfume smells **slightly strange**
Adverbial	It's **up the road** • She looks **as if she's been partying all night** He sounds **like a horse** when he eats • This tortilla tastes **like rubber**
Noun phrase	He is **a complete fool** • The crumble turned out **a success** She became **a successful lawyer** • He proved **a reliable defender**

● Object complements: transitive verbs

Adjective	We ate it **fresh** • She considers him **too thick** for the job We found the weather **unbearable** • Squash it **flat**
Adverbial	They took the crumpets **out of the breadbin** She didn't keep her feet **on the ground**
Preposition + verb -ing	They accused me **of breaking** the stapler • I prevented him **from entering** They charged us **for parking** behind the pub • I thanked her **for coming**
Non-finite verb	He felt something **crawling up his leg** They require it **to be done** immediately • She likes them **fried**

● that/Ø complements

After reporting verbs	She suggested **that I should freeze the figs** I told her **that she was too late**
After verbs of cognition	He believed **that the enemy had retreated** • I know **Ø you are hiding there** I realised **that someone was trying to dazzle me**
After verbs of perception	She noticed **that the door was unlocked** • I saw **that she had been crying** We observed **that he was nervous** • I heard **that he had been sacked**

● wh- complements

After verbs of cognition	I wonder **where they are** • Can you guess **who's coming to dinner**? I don't know **what he wants** • I don't believe **what you just said**
After reporting verbs	Did they say **when they were arriving**? • She told me **how to do it** Will you ask them **why they want it**? • Do you know **whether he's asleep**?

● Adjective complements

that-clause	It's strange **that they haven't left a message** It's interesting **that the dog only barks at your friends**
wh- clause	I'm not certain **what I'm supposed to do** She's quite sure **where she wants to study**
Prepositional phrase	He's quite knowledgeable **about mechanics** She's very good **with rabbits** • He's pretty bad **at dancing**
to infinitive	The guinea-pigs are really difficult **to catch** His strokes are lovely **to watch** • I'm so glad **to see you**
-ing verb	These milk cartons aren't worth **keeping** • It's exciting **seeing** you again It was nice **meeting** you • It's hopeless **waiting** for him to reply

Co-ordination

● Coordination of word classes and clause elements

Adjective + adjective	She is an **unsociable yet intelligent** person
Adverb + adverb	She arranged the flowers **quickly but carefully**
Auxiliary + auxiliary	She **is, or was,** living in the suburbs
Full verb + full verb	He **sat and read** the paper all morning
Modal + modal	We **can and must** succeed
Non-finite + non-finite	I saw him **running, then slowing down**
Noun + noun	**Roses and tulips** are my favourite flowers
Noun phrase + noun phrase	He was wearing **a blue shirt and green trousers**
Predicate + predicate	They **went into the garden and sat on a bench**
Preposition + preposition	It was impossible to pass **over or under** the fence
Prep phrase + prep phrase	He was not sitting **under the table, but on it**
Pronoun + pronoun	**He and I** went to the same university
Relative clause + relative clause	Jean, **who is French and speaks German,** works in a bank

● Double co-ordination

(Prepositional phrase + prepositional phrase) x 2	He went **to Germany by ship and to Italy by train**
(Indirect object + direct object) x 2	I sent **Joel a CD and Steve a dictionary**
(Object + complement) x 2	They painted **the kitchen blue and the hall green**

● Ellipsis: segregatory co-ordination (separable elements)

Complements of the same verb	She seems **proud but lonely**
Objects of the same verb	They broke **the fence and a window**
Subjects of the same verb	**Jose and Maria** were having a drink
Verbs with the same subject	Dracula **lay down and sighed**
Verbs with the same object	He **rinsed and dried** his hair

● Ellipsis: combinatory co-ordination (inseparable elements)

Inseparable adverbs	I see them **now and then**
Inseparable complements	He left the kitchen **spick and span**
Inseparable objects	I think we should stick **the cardboard and the paper** together
Inseparable subjects	**Ahmed and Abdullah** make a highly effective partnership
Inseparable verbs	Can you stop **to-ing and fro-ing**?

● Correlatives

as ... as	He is **as kind as he is intemperate**
both ... and	**Both kangaroos and possums** are marsupials
either ... or	We can **either throw it away or give it to charity**
if ... or	I don't know **if she prefers carrots or parsnips**
neither ... nor	I like **neither red nor yellow** plums
not only ... but ... also	She **not only plays chess but is also an outstanding archer**

Types of Question

● Direct yes/no questions

With primary verbs:	*Am* I annoying you? • *Are* you comfortable? • *Is* she in town? • *Do* you smoke? *Does* she like it? • *Did* they get there? • *Have* they got back yet? • *Has* he finished it?
With modals	*Can* you swim? • *Could* she see? • *Will* they come? • *Would* he do such a thing? *Shall* I ring? • *Should* we call her? • *Must* you do that? • *May* we go now?
Quantity: possession and existence	Have you got *any* soya sauce? • Is there *much* snow in the winter? Does she have *many* siblings? • Are there *any* good films on at the moment?
Quantity: requests and offers	Can I have *some* cake? • May we take *a few* biscuits? Will you let me have *a little* milk? • Could you make *some* custard?
Indefinite entities	Did you want to see *anyone* in particular? • Are you going *anywhere* exciting? Are you buying *anything* for Martha? • Are you going to tell *anyone*?
Experience or completion	Have you *ever* been to China? • Did you *ever* hear of such a thing? Have you visited the ruins *yet*? • Have you done the carpets *yet*?
Negative	*Don't* you want to see the ducks? • *Haven't* you done enough drumming? *Won't* you stay for dinner? • *Couldn't* you be a little more polite?

● Direct *wh-* questions

Subject	*Who* told the police? • *What* made that awful noise?
Direct Object	*Who(m)* did you see? • *What* have you found? • *Who* are they going to promote?
Indirect Object	*Who* did you give it to? • *Which company* did you send it to?
Subject Complement	*What colour* is it? • *What* does it taste *like*? • *Whose* papers are these?
Object Complement	*What* did you call me? • *How* do you prefer it? • *What* did you make him do?
Adverbial: time	*When* do you feed the hamster? • *What time* will you eat? • *What day* is she coming?
Adverbial: frequency	*How often* should we wash the curtains? • *How frequently* do you shave?
Adverbial: measure	*How long* is the lecture? • *How far* is it to the centre? • *How much* do you want?
Adverbial: place	*Where* do you go on Friday nights? • *Whereabouts* did they find the missing girl?
Adverbial: reason	*Why* didn't you leave the keys? • *Whyever* would they do that? • *Why not* sell it?
Adverbial: process	*How* does she sing? • *However* did you manage that? • *How* could we get it?

● Indirect questions: affirmative word order in subordinate clause

Do you think	he did it? • they have any chance? • she wants to come? • the government will resign?
Do you know	where the bank is? • if the trains are running? • why she resigned? • what he said?
Have you any idea	why this gadget won't work? • how I can get to the airport? • what this means?

● Cleft questions

Yes/no	Was it Mr. Snaggs you wanted to see? • Is it on Saturday you're going?
Wh-	Where is it he went on holiday? • What was it she saw? • Who is it that's coming?

● Question tags

You live [*do* live] in Glasgow	*don't* you?	We *weren't* quick enough,	*were* we?
He works [*does* work] in Leeds,	*doesn't* he?	You *can* drive,	*can't* you?
She won [*did* win] the race,	*didn't* she?	They *might* come,	*mightn't* they?
You *haven't* started yet,	*have* you?	They *could* have phoned,	*couldn't* they?
She *hadn't* even got up,	*had* she?	You'*ll* let me know,	*won't* you?
He has [*does* have] to stop,	*doesn't* he?	She *should* take the job,	*shouldn't* she?
She had [*did* have] some trouble,	*didn't* she?	He *wouldn't* leave her,	*would* he?
You'*re* making fun of me,	*aren't* you?	You *used* [*did* use] to play chess,	*didn't* you?

● Echo questions

A: I'*m* a doctor.	B: *Are* you?	A: I ate [*did* eat] it.	B: *Did* you?
A: I'*ve never* seen the Queen.	B: *Haven't you?*	A: They *won't* do it!	B: *Won't* they?
A: I'*d* like to go to sleep.	B: *Would* you?	A: I *don't* believe him.	B: *Don't* you?

Questions with *How*: quantity and measure

How **ancient**	is that monument?
How **big**	are your marrows?
How **deep**	is Loch Ness?
How **dense**	is mercury?
How **expensive**	was that diamond ring?
How **far**	is it from Cambridge to London?
How **fast**	is your new car?
How **heavy**	is your luggage?
How **high**	is Mont Blanc?
How **long**	is the living-room?
How **long**	does the film last?
How **many**	do you want?
How **many**	people were there?
How **much**	does it cost?
How **much**	milk do you want?
How **much**	are you overdrawn?
How **old**	are your children?
How **rich**	is the chairman of the company?
How **strong**	is this medicine?
How **tall**	is your brother?
How **thick**	is the package?
How **wide**	is the Amazon?

Questions with *What* + noun: category, quantity and measure

What **age**	did he start school?
What **form**	do his fits take?
What **fraction**	of the population smokes?
What **kind of**	sweets do you like?
What **percentage**	did interest rates rise by?
What **pressure**	are the tyres?
What **proportion**	of the audience is female?
What **shape**	is the swimming pool?
What **size**	chair legs do we need?
What **sort of**	celebration are you having for your birthday?
What **speed**	should I set it on?
What **strength**	is the mixture?
What **temperature**	should the water be?
What **time**	are they arriving?
What **type of**	screws do we need to put up this shelf?
What **volume**	did you put it on?

Mood

● Positive declarative mood

Factual	*The fish **are** hungry • Everybody **went** home*
Opinion	*I **agree** with you • I **hate** mackerel*
Emphatic	*I **<u>did</u> pay** for the drinks • They **do** drink tea*
Promise	*I **shall make** sure you get your money*

● Negative declarative mood (*not*)

Factual	*There **aren't** any peas in the freezer*
Opinion	*I **don't think** it makes any difference*
Emphatic	*I **have <u>not</u> given** away your lousy secrets*
Promise	*I **won't drop** it again*

● Nuclear negatives

No	*And **no** birds sang • I've had **no** sleep*
Nothing	***Nothing** ever happens in Bland Street • I know **nothing***
Nobody/no-one	***Nobody** has any information • He's speaking to **no-one***
Nowhere	***Nowhere** is better than Barton • They're going **nowhere***

● Interrogative mood

Polar (*Yes/No*)	***Do you** want some tea? • **Can you** stop interrupting, please?*
Alternative	***Would you** like it in bed **or** downstairs? • **Are you** tired **or** just bored?*
Subjective	***Who** asked for blackberry tart with custard? • **What** happened?*
Objective	***What** did you buy for your mum? • **Who** did she find?*
Prepositional objective	***Where** did they get it **from**? • **What** did you mix it **with**?*
Adverbial	***How** did they react to her performance? • **When** do you bath?*

● Imperative mood

Base form	***Leave**! • **Go** away! • **Fetch** the runner beans*
Do + base form	***Do be** careful! • **Don't snore**! • **Do help** yourself to nibbles*
You + base form	***You ask** • **You lay** the table • **You find** the flea powder*
Let + object + base form	***Let me get** you some dry clothes • **Let them come** in*

● Exclamative mood (*What/How* + clause element)

Subject	***What strange people** inhabit these parts! • **What big ships** anchor in this port!*
Complement	***How interesting** your life is! • Lord, **what fools** these mortals be*
Adverb	***How fast** she runs! • **How hard** he has fallen!*
Object	***What a big sausage** I've eaten! • **What great tunes** you play!*

● Subjunctive mood

wish + were	*I wish I **were** in France • She wishes she **were** less critical*
if + were	*If I **were** you I'd give him a piece of my mind*
Mandative subjunctive: subject + base form	*I propose that he **submit** his plans by the 12th* *I insist that you **attend** the next meeting* *It is imperative that we **take** precautions* *We made a decision that the tulips **be** planted in rows*
Formulaic subjunctive: base form in various word-order patterns	*Heaven **forbid** that any harm **befall** them* *We'll go on digging **come** what may* ***Suffice** it to say that the only food was pasta* ***Be** that as it may, we still need to improve security*

Marked Sentence Structures

● Inversion: adverbial + auxiliary + subject + full verb (or *be* + subject)

Never (+ Present Perfect/Past Perfect)	*have I seen* such extraordinary roses
On no account (+ Modal)	*must you forget* to warn her
No sooner (+ Past Perfect + *than*)	*had I arrived* than the guinea-pig expired
Only when she winked (+ Past Simple)	*did I realise* she was joking
Little (+ Present Simple/Past Simple)	*does he realise* that we'll be waiting for him
Not until she rang (+ Past Simple)	*did we hear* the news
Hardly (+ Past Perfect + *when*)	*had I got up* when the neighbour called
Not a soul (+ Present Perfect/Past Simple)	*have we encountered* in this miserable town
Seldom/Rarely/Hardly ever (+ Present Simple)	*do we see* golden eagles in this region
In no circumstances (+ will/shall/can)	*will I accept* responsibility for his behaviour
On no account (+ must/should)	*must you touch* this knob
Nowhere (else) (+ will/Present Perfect)	*will you see* such perfect examples of spiders' webs
In no way (+ is it true/is it the case)	*is it* true that intelligence has a genetic basis
Such (+ *be* + noun phrase)	*was her efficiency* that she finished in half an hour

● Inversion: repositioning of object/complement/adverbial; inversion of subject and verb

Really delicious	*were* the figs in brandy
Sitting on the bed	*was* an enormous Cheshire cat
Up	*went* the kite
Worst of all	*was* the singing
To Fred	*came* the realisation that he would never win the prize

● Fronting: repositioning of object/complement/adverbial; no inversion

Where we're going to sleep	I have no idea
Since 1997	we've had to manage on state benefit
How he reached that conclusion	I cannot tell
These	I want to keep
Over the grey, rubbish-strewn city	the ravenous blackbirds flew

● Clefting: *It* + *be* + clause element + *who/whom/which/that/Ø* + clause

Focus on subject	It was **John** who gave Barry the gun
Focus on direct object	It's **fish** we need for supper this evening
Focus on indirect object	It was **Jane** I sent the flowers to
Focus on adverbial	It was **at three o'clock** that the procession started

● Pseudo-clefting: *What* + subject + verb + *be* + object/complement/clause

Focus on direct object	What I don't know is **when they're coming**
Focus on nominal clause	What I've found is **that these sheep never wander far**
Focus on subject complement	What I really like are **chocolate drops**
Focus on non-finite clause	What I really want to do is **have a nice cool shower**

● Pseudo-clefting: *The one/time/place/reason/person/way*, etc.

The person I'd most like to meet is the chief • **The thing** I don't understand is why she never phoned
The time he comes home is 6.30 • **The sauce** I like the most is made of stinking fish
The place I really remember is Acapulco • **The country** I'd most like to visit is Pakistan
The reason I told you to leave was that it was dangerous • **The one programme** I like is the news
The way I carve it is like this • **The best tactic to employ** is to catch them on the break

Punctuation

● Comma

After non-finite *-ing* clause (reason)	***Feeling tired,*** *she lay on the sofa.* ***Not having any luck with the Joneses,*** *we tried the Robinsons.*
After salutations	*Dear Ms Lipswich,* • *Dear Sir or Madam,* • *Yours sincerely,*
After sentence-linking adverbial	*He has a bad heel.* **However,** *he still goes for walks.* *Oil reserves are depleted.* **Moreover,** *gas supplies are running low.* *I lost the race.* **Still,** *I enjoyed the experience.*
Before quotation mark and reporting verb	*"We're so glad to see you,"* **said Gemma.** *"There are no oranges,"* **said the fruiterer.**
Before *so*	*I didn't have much money,* **so I couldn't get any flowers.** *I won't know until tomorrow,* **so I'll tell you then.**
Before *with* + *-ing* clauses	*Jones won the championship,* **with the second prize going to Thorsen.** *The two ships separated,* **with Insania sailing off to the Scilly Isles.**
Beginning and end of non-defining appositive phrases	*Newnham,* **the poshest part of Cambridge,** *has no betting shop.* *Rakespeare,* **the well-known gardener,** *also writes poetry.*
Beginning and end of non-defining relative clauses	*Leeds,* **which is in Yorkshire,** *has an annual carnival.* *John,* **whose ambition is to be a doctor,** *is doing his A-levels.*
Between subordinate clause and main clause	***When you come into the hall,*** *turn left.* ***Unless prices go down,*** *nobody will be able to afford it.*
Change of topic after *and* and *but*	*He has gone to Australia,* **and nobody knows when he is coming back.** *The fence fell over,* **but it's not our fault.**
Horizontal lists	*She won't eat* **chicken, cheese, prawns** *or butter.* *He* **stroked the cat, hummed a tune, sat down** *and opened a book.*
Separating adjectives before a noun	*a* **colourless, odourless** *gas* *three* **thickset, sinister-looking** *men*

● No comma

After subject	*The man who lives in the next house* **Ø** *is a lawyer.*	
Between main clause and non-finite *-ing* clause	*He came into the room* **Ø** *whistling a tune.* *The bird sat on a branch* **Ø** *warbling.*	
Between main clause and subordinate clause	*Turn left* **Ø** *when you come into the hall.* *Nobody will be able to afford it* **Ø** *unless prices go down.*	
Vertical lists	*Three eggs* *A plucked plover* *A sprig of parsley*	*Collect jacket* *Buy stamps* *Order new teapot*

● Variable usage

Before *and* at the end of a list	*We bought three cups, two plates,* **and a bowl.** *We bought three cups, two plates* **Ø** *and a bowl.*
Times and dates at the beginning of a sentence	***In 1921,*** *the Russian civil war came to an end.* ***In 1921*** **Ø** *the Russian civil war came to an end.*

● Colon

After names in dramatised dialogue	*Alison: I refuse to accept your apologies.* *Geoffrey: Please listen to me!*
After reporting verb and before direct speech	*The glazier* **said:** *"That window needs replacing."* *Mr. Danks* **declared:** *"This picnic's going to be a wild success."*
Before a list of examples	*She speaks four languages: French, Greek, Hindi and Russian.* *We could describe him in several ways: mendacious, cunning, subtle...*
Forward reference	*This is the plan: we creep round the back, climb over the wall and...*

● Semi-colon

Coordinating two independent clauses	*The tightrope walker wobbled; the crowd gasped.* *The plans have been finalised; now it is time to put them into practice.*
Listing of coordinated items	*The contents consist of three sets of tables and chairs; a piano and stool; four cups and saucers; and a porcelain bird in a cage.*

Punctuation (continued)

● Capital letter

Acronyms	*the UAE • NATO • ASLEF • the UN • the BBC*
Days, months, festivals	*Tuesday • Thursday • Ramadan • Maundy Thursday • April • October*
Languages	*Hebrew • Sanskrit • Welsh • Akkadian*
Personal titles and names	*Sir Jack Stirrup • Mrs. Coolson • Professor Akensop*
Place names	*Ulan Bator • Lake Superior • Red Square • Egypt • Stone Street*
Start of sentence	*The trust between our nations has been sundered at a stroke.* *Nobody would say that she has a passive personality.*
Titles of books, films, etc. **(1ˢᵗ word + content words)**	*War and Peace • Chrysanthemums • The Flight of the Bumblebee* *A Dream of Red Mansions • Poplars • Children's Games*

● Full stop

Before quotation mark	*"There are no foxes in the vicinity."*
Separating sentences which are linked with an adverbial	*The flat was really expensive.* **However**, *we managed to get a loan.* *He says he's a bit tired.* **In other words**, *he's exhausted.*

● Question mark

After questions	*Did you see the rainbow?* *Where did they find that extraordinary wallpaper?*
After question tags	*We haven't got the wrong day,* **have we?** *She will get on the right train,* **won't she?**

● Exclamation mark

After exclamations beginning ***What*** **and** ***How***	*What an extraordinary opening goal!* *How strange that he should suddenly appear after all this time!*
Imperatives	*Leave the room at once! Stop flicking your hair!*

● Hyphen

In some compound nouns	**washing-machine • son-in-law • dry-cleaner • baby-sitter • six-pack** **ex-husband • down-and-out • passer-by • make-believe**
In compound attributive adjectives and modifiers	*a* **well-dressed** *youth • a* **highly-paid** *executive • a* **single-minded** *careerist* *a* **red-light** *district •* **anti-abortion** *campaigners*

● No hyphen

In compound adjectives used predicatively	*He is* **well dressed** *• They are* **badly paid** *• He is* **recently promoted** *Your opinions are* **clearly expressed** *• I was* **deeply impressed**

● Quotation marks

Direct speech	*"We are about to witness a historic event," announced the President.* *Joe said: "The fact is, we will have to walk home."*

● Dash/brackets

Asides/incidental information	*The king –* **the old one, that is** *– had recently shaved off his beard.* *When you see Fred* **(the one with the curly hair)**, *tell him to call me.*

● Apostrophe

After business names	*We bought it in* **Hanbury's** *• Shall we meet at* **Siddle's?**
Contractions	**I've** *won •* **It's** *2.00 •* **I'd** *like two pieces •* **They're** *completely mad*
Plural genitive (irregular)	*the* **mice's** *tails • the* **oxen's** *horns •* **women's** *clothes*
Plural genitive (regular)	*the* **cats'** *whiskers • the* **ships'** *masts • my* **brothers'** *fights*
Singular genitive	*the* **dog's** *food •* **William's** *teeth • my* **friend's** *holiday*

● No apostrophe

Plurals	**tomatoes • chips • avocados • magazines**
Possessive pronouns	*These courgettes are* **ours** *•* **Theirs** *are the straggly ones • Where's* **its** *tail?*

● Variable usage

Numerical decades	*the* **1930s** *• the* **1930's**

Analysis of sentence types

For each sentence below, the **class** of each word is given, together with the **type** within each class, and the **form** where it is variable. Within the **phrase types**, the verb phrase may be divided by an adverb, as in sentences 2 and 3. A clause, whether independent or subordinate, may have another clause embedded within it, as in sentences 2 and 3. This is indicated by square brackets [ ]

1. *Our little dog always licks the plates clean after dinner.* (Simple sentence)
2. *Our little dog always licks the plates clean after dinner and then goes into the living-room to lie down.* (Compound sentence)
3. *Our little dog always licks the plates clean after dinner unless we're entertaining guests he's never met before.* (Complex sentence)

Sentence 1

	Our	*little*	*dog*	*always*	*licks*	*the*	*plates*	*clean*	*after*	*dinner*
Word class	determiner	adjective	noun	adverb	verb	determiner	noun	adjective	preposition	noun
Type	possessive	classifying	countable	frequency	full + transitive	article	countable	qualitative	sequence	countable
Form	1pp		singular		present 3ps	definite	plural			singular
Phrase type	Noun P			Adverb P	Verb P ('Present Simple')	Noun P		Adjective P	[Prep P [Noun P]]	
Clause element	Subject			Adverb	Verb	Direct object		Complement (obj)	Adverb	
Clause type	Independent finite clause →									

Sentence 2, second part

	and	*then*	*goes*	*into*	*the*	*living-room*	*to lie*	*down*
Word class	conjunction	adverb	verb	preposition	determiner	noun	verb	adverb
Type	co-ordinating	sequence	full + intransitive	direction	article	countable	phrasal verb + intrans	
Form			present 3ps		definite	singular	infinitive	
Phrase type		Adverb P	Verb P ('Present Simple')	Prepositional P			Verb P (non-finite)	
Clause element		Adverb	Verb	Adverb			Adverb	
Clause type	← [Independent finite clause [non-finite clause]] →						Non-finite clause →	

Sentence 3, second part

	unless	*we*	*'re (are)*	*entertaining*	*guests*	*ø (whom)*	*he*	*'s (has)*	*never*	*met*	*before*
Word class	conjunction	pronoun	verb	verb	noun	pronoun	pronoun	verb	adverb	verb	adverb
Type	subordinating	subject	primary	full + trans	countable	relative (object)	subject	primary	frequency	full + trans	anteriority
Form		1pp	present 1pp	-ing form	plural	zero	3ps	present 3ps		past part. irr	
Phrase type		Noun P	Verb P (Present Progressive)		Noun P	Noun P	← Noun P →	Verb P (Present Perfective) + Adverb P			Adverb P
Clause element		Subject	Verb		Object		Subject	Verb + Adverb			Adverb
Clause type	← [Subordinate adverbial clause [Defining relative clause]]						Defining relative clause →				

3ps = third person singular   1pp = first person plural   Square brackets [ ] indicate embedding of a phrase or clause

Note on terminology

The terminology of English grammar is not always as transparent as it might be, particularly since there is no general agreement on specific terms. Some grammar books use the term 'Present Continuous', while others prefer 'Present Progressive'; the easily understandable 'Yes/no questions' are sometimes referred to as the somewhat icy 'Polar Interrogatives'; and 'Sentence-linking adverbials' usually become 'Link words' or 'Linkers' in the English language classroom. There seems to be tension between terms which are conveniently descriptive, and those which, because of their Latin origins, exude an academic aura.

But how descriptive are the apparently descriptive terms? It is not at all clear what is simple about the Present Simple. If it is the fact that the form consists of only one verb, then this is clearly not true of the Present Perfect Simple (two verbs) or the Future Perfect Simple (three verbs). If it is something to do with the mode and time of action denoted by a verb in the Present Simple, then we are forced to conclude that *I occasionally wash the clothes between 3.00 and 5.00 on a Wednesday afternoon* is somehow simpler in concept than a sentence using an aspectual verb form, such as the Present Continuous/Present Progressive *I'm eating an orange*. And what exactly does the 'Perfect' in 'Present Perfect' mean? Literally, it denotes an action which has been 'perfected', in other words completed. (We might well ask why the Present Perfect isn't called the Present Complete, since outside the field of grammar nobody ever uses the word 'perfect' in the sense of 'complete'). Yet in many examples of the Present Perfect, the action is demonstrably not complete: *I have eaten beans for several years; He has worked in London since January*. In fact, many foreign learners of English are convinced that the Present Perfect always denotes an uncompleted action. We can thus unequivocally state that the term 'perfect' is worse than useless in enhancing understanding of this verb form.

When we consider conditional sentences, the labelling seems perfectly straightforward: First Conditional, Second Conditional, Third Conditional. That is, until we come to the Zero Conditional. It would seem that this form was only discovered after all the others. Or is it that the second part of a sentence such as *If I feel hungry in the mornings, I usually buy a sandwich* is based on a zero condition, whatever that is? If so, then we are obliged, in the interests of consistency, to say that the second part of *If it rains, I'll stay indoors* is based on a first condition, which is clearly nonsensical. Of course, there is no real reason why numbering shouldn't work: we could just as easily talk about Present 1 and Present 2 as about Present Simple and Present Continuous/Progressive, although the term 'Present' might still be a problem, since these forms are frequently used to denote future actions.

Another problem of terminology occurs when we consider the major levels of grammar: word class, phrase, clause. Once we know what a noun is and what a phrase is, we can easily work out what a noun phrase is: a group of words with a noun as its central feature. When we use nouns and noun phrases in clauses, however, we must call them subjects, objects or complements in order to show what their function is. This seems perfectly reasonable. But if we now take another word class, that of verbs, things start to become confusing. We can have a verb such as *fly* and use it as the main element of the verb phrases *would fly*, *was flying*, etc. When we wish to specify the function of verbs and verb phrase in clauses, however, we are forced to use the same term again: 'verb'; forced, that is, if we follow the example of most mainstream grammar books. The result of this is that anyone who is trying to come to grips with grammar for the first time may well confuse 'verb' as a word class with 'verb' as a clause element.

Even more confusing are adverbs and adverbials: an adverb is a single word, while an adverbial is a single word or group of words with an adverbial function, though it is not an adverb phrase, which consists solely of adverbs, and an adverb (again) is a clause element with an adverbial function. Inconsistency is not only a feature of terminology here, but also of substance: why, if a noun phrase can consist of a noun preceded or followed by other word classes and phrases, does a verb phrase consist solely of verbs and an adverb phrase solely of adverbs?

One of the most problematical terms regarding clause structure is 'complement', which literally means 'something which completes'. The copular verbs (poetic term!) *be, seem, appear, taste* require a noun, noun phrase or adjective after them, as in the sentence *He is a doctor*, and this is called a 'subject complement' because it says something about the subject *He*. In the sentence *They elected him secretary*, the complement *secretary* says something about the object *him* and is thus an 'object complement'. Other verbs such as *hit, take, buy, make* require an object after them: *Her car hit the crash barrier*: the object is in some way affected by the action, in contrast to the complement, which says something about the subject or object. So far so good. Yet the verbs *hit, take, buy, make* must all be 'completed' with an object, just as the verbs *be, seem, appear, taste* must be 'completed' with a complement. In this sense, therefore, objects are just as much complements as complements are. The question thus arises as to why the affective function of an object is apparently more important than its complementary function, whereas the complementary function of a complement seems to take precedence over its other functions in a clause.

Many of the problems of grammatical terminology have arisen because of the history of grammar itself. Every generation has reacted to the terminology of a previous one and produced its own terms, without, in many cases, adding anything significant to the understanding of the concepts involved. The result is a mishmash of semi-description, illogical enumeration and outright mislabelling. Despite this, the English grammar system manages somehow to be accessible and describable to anyone wishing to understand it. The following glossary of grammatical terms is intended to help in the understanding of items in the tables which may not initially appear to be clear.

Glossary

Active voice: The action of a verb in the active voice comes from the SUBJECT: *She* [subject] *plays the piano* • *They* [subject] *laughed.* Compare PASSIVE.

Adjective: A word which typically modifies a NOUN, either before it, as in *the **green** shirt*, or after a COPULAR VERB: *The room is/seems/looks **untidy**.* Most adjectives can be preceded by an ADVERB: *very strange* • *extremely clever* and have a COMPARATIVE form: ***stronger** • **bigger** • **more expensive***
See tables on pp.16, 17, 18.

Adverb: A word that modifies 1) a VERB: *run **quickly*** 2) an ADJECTIVE: ***really** nice* 3) another adverb: ***rather** loudly* or 4) a CLAUSE: ***Overall**, they performed well.* See tables on pp.52, 53.

Adverbial: Any word or structure which can function as a MODIFIER of a CLAUSE or CLAUSE ELEMENT, in particular the VERB PHRASE: ***The way I see it**, this war is a total mistake* • *He listened **extremely attentively**.*

Agent: The performer of an act or the experiencer of a state. The agent can be the SUBJECT of a verb in the ACTIVE VOICE: ***The cat** was sleeping* or the OBJECT of the preposition *by* in the PASSIVE VOICE: *Hamlet was written by **Shakespeare.***

Article: 1) Definite: ***the** table* 2) Indefinite: ***a** fish* • ***an** elephant*.

Aspect: In combination with a TENSE, a verb form which indicates progression (Progressive) or completion (Perfective):
1) Progressive (or continuous): *She is sleeping* (present) • *They were playing* (past)
2) Perfective: *I have won* (present) • *He had forgotten* (past)
3) Progressive perfective: *We have been jogging* (present) • *She had been working* (past).

Base form: The form of the verb from which all other forms are derived, either with the addition of an ending: ***arrive**, arriv**ed**, arriv**ing**;* or with an internal change of form ***eat**, **ate**.*

Clause: A group of words typically containing a SUBJECT and a VERB, which may form a complete sentence: *He entered the room* or be the MAIN part of a two-part (COMPLEX) sentence: ***I'll come down** when I'm ready* or be a SUBORDINATE part of a sentence: ***If it rains** I'll cry.* There are also NON-FINITE clauses, which contain a verb without a subject: *... being late for work... • ... exhausted by the long hours ...* and verbless clauses: *Unhappy about her purchases...* See tables on pp.62, 63, 64.

Clause element: There are five clause elements: SUBJECT, VERB, OBJECT, COMPLEMENT, ADVERBIAL. See the table of clause structures on p.62 for the various combinations of these elements.

Cleft sentence: A sentence made up of two CLAUSES deriving from a simpler one-clause sentence and beginning *It...* The simple sentence *Susan went to London* can be clefted to become *It was Susan* [clause 1] *who went to London* [clause 2]. A **pseudo-cleft** sentence begins with a NOMINAL CLAUSE (*what*-clause) operating as SUBJECT: *What Susan did* [nominal clause] *was to go to London* [main clause]. See table on p.70.

Comparative: A form of ADJECTIVE or ADVERB typically used with *than* to indicate a comparison: *These shoes are **smaller** than yours* • *He runs **faster** than me.* See table on p.18.

Complement: A word or phrase which gives information about the SUBJECT of a COPULAR VERB: *This soup* [subject] *tastes **rather salty*** or the OBJECT of a TRANSITIVE VERB: *We consider him* [object] ***the best candidate for the job.*** See table on p.65.

Complex sentence: A sentence consisting of a main CLAUSE and a SUBORDINATE or dependent clause, linked by a subordinating CONJUNCTION such as *if, when, because, although, before*. See table on p.74.

Compound sentence: A sentence consisting of two independent CLAUSES linked by a coordinating CONJUNCTION such as *and, but, or*. See table on p.74.

Conjunction: 1) subordinating: a word which links a SUBORDINATE CLAUSE to a MAIN CLAUSE: ***If** you drink that milk* [subordinate clause] *we won't have any left* [main clause]. See table on p.62
2) coordinating: a word which links two independent clauses: *They met in the park* [clause 1] ***and** had a cup of tea* [clause 2]. See table on p.66.

Coordination: The linking of two members of the same word class, or two PHRASES, or two CLAUSES with a coordinating CONJUNCTION: *Fish and chips* (noun + noun) • *over hill and down dale* (prepositional phrase + prepositional phrase) • *We'll watch TV or play cards* (clause + clause). See table on p.66.

Correlatives: Pairs of linking words which have an emphasising function: ***both** John **and** Stephen* • ***either** green **or** red* • ***neither** well **nor** badly* • ***not (only)** on Saturdays **but (also)** on Sundays.* They can be used with the full range of CLAUSE ELEMENTS.

Copular verb: A verb which is followed by a noun or adjective COMPLEMENT giving information about the SUBJECT: *She **seems** intelligent • He **is** a doctor • This **tastes** nice.* See table on p.44.

Countable noun: A noun which, in its plural form, can be preceded by a number: *three **penguins** • two **people*** or, in its singular form, by the indefinite article: *a **cake** • an **elephant**.* See table on p.6.

Demonstrative: 1) PRONOUNS: *I don't want **this/that/these/those*** 2) DETERMINERS (before nouns): ***this** hat • **that** table • **these** books • **those** houses.*

Derivation: A change of form involving a change of word class: *photograph → photographic* (noun to adjective) • *playful → playfully* (adjective to adverb). See also INFLECTION. See table on p.21.

Determiner: A word that defines the scope, quantity or reference of the noun or noun phrase it precedes. See table on p.9 for the different types.

Dynamic verb: A verb denoting actions, events, processes or utterances: *He **jumped** over the fence • She **sneezed** • They were **waiting** • He **said** he liked fish.* See table on p.23.

Ellipsis: The omission of a word or words from a sentence, often occurring in a response, in order to avoid repetition: *A: Do you play tennis? B: Yes, I do **(play tennis)**.*

Ergative verb: A verb which can be used both intransitively and transitively, where the subject of the INTRANSITIVE can be the object of the TRANSITIVE: *The door* [subject] *closed • Someone closed the door* [object]. See table on p.44.

Finite: A form of the verb which requires a SUBJECT: *He **eats** fast • They **have gone** • We **won't tell** you.* See table of verb phrases on p.60 for the full list. See also NON-FINITE.

Fronting: Fronting involves the shifting of a CLAUSE ELEMENT to the beginning of the sentence, but without the INVERSION of SUBJECT and VERB: ***Where he's been all this time** I've no idea • **Those** we'll throw away.* See table on p.70.

Head: The nucleus of a PHRASE. In a noun phrase, the head is the noun around which all the other elements are grouped: *The old **man** with the red tie.* In a prepositional phrase, the head is the preposition at the beginning of the phrase: ***under** the bed.* In a verb phrase it is the main verb: *having **seen** • was **eaten**.* See tables on pp.57, 58.

Infinitive: The form of the verb consisting of *to* + BASE FORM: *to be, to play, to arrive.*

Inflection: A change of form within a word class: *go → goes* (verb) • *my → mine* (pronoun) • *dog → dogs* (noun). See also DERIVATION. See table on p.5.

Interrogative: The order AUXILIARY + SUBJECT + (AUXILIARY) + MAIN VERB used to form questions: ***Did you see** them? • **Have they phoned** yet? • **Has he been arrested**?* See table on p.67.

Intransitive: A verb which has no direct OBJECT and no COMPLEMENT: *She **sighed** • I **resign** • I can't **stop**.* Many verbs can be used both transitively and intransitively. See table on p.44.

Inversion: The reversal of the positions of SUBJECT and AUXILIARY VERB in a sentence: *Not only **has he** passed his exams, he has also got into university.* See table on p.70.

Main clause: A clause which can operate independently as a complete sentence, but which may be linked to a SUBORDINATE CLAUSE.

Marked sentence structures: A marked sentence structure is one where the normal order of a declarative sentence (see MOOD) has been changed in order to add special emphasis or to highlight a particular element. See table on p.70 for the different types.

Modal auxiliary verb: Verbs such as *can, must, will, may* which convey a range of meanings expressing the speaker's attitude towards an event or circumstance. See table on p.29.

Modifier: A word, PHRASE or CLAUSE that modifies the meaning of the NOUN, ADJECTIVE or VERB that it precedes (pre-modifier): ***green** jelly • **really** nice • **never** smoke*; or that it follows (post-modifier): • *the pen **on the table** • the hat **she was wearing**.* See table on p.57.

Mood: Mood indicates the basic type of utterance being made by the speaker: declarative, negative, interrogative, imperative, exclamative or subjunctive. It can be indicated by word order, the form of the verb or the addition of other elements, typically negative words and auxiliary verbs. See table on p.69 for examples.

Nominal clause: A clause typically introduced by *that* or *what* that contains a VERB PHRASE as its nucleus and which can function as the SUBJECT of a verb: ***That he is very capable** is indisputable*; or the direct OBJECT: *I know **what you want**.* See table on p.63.

Non-finite: A form of the VERB which does not take a SUBJECT and which does not, in itself form a TENSE.
1) infinitive: ***to fly** • to sleep* 2) present participle: *I saw you **running*** 3) past participle: ***Exhausted**, she fell asleep immediately.* See table on p.60 for combinations of non-finite forms.

Noun: A word that names or denotes or labels or refers to objects (*table, stone, roof*), properties (*hardness, malleability*), creatures (*owl, dragon, wolf*), types of people (*fool, inspector, child*), abstractions (*intelligence, bravery*), etc. See table on p.6 for a wider range of categories.

Object: The object of a verb is either the PATIENT: *He broke the **vase*** [direct object], or the RECIPIENT: *She gave **me*** [indirect object] *the money*. See table on p.44.

Orientation: The relationship between the speaker of an utterance and 1) his or her surroundings 2) present, past or future time 3) other people. Sometimes referred to as 'deixis'. See table on p.15.

Participle: See NON-FINITE.

Particle: 1) A word used in the formation of a PHRASAL VERB: *get **up** • take **away** • bring **about***. These words are mostly identical to PREPOSITIONS, but have an ADVERBIAL function. See table on p.33. 2) The word *to* used before the BASE FORM of the verb to form the INFINITIVE: ***to** stop*.

Partitive: An expression with a quantifying function which applies to a particular type of thing or substance: *a **pinch** of salt • a **grain** of sand*. See table on p.13.

Passive form: A compound form of the verb consisting of the verb *be* in one of its forms together with the Past PARTICIPLE: *is played • has been seen • will be taken*. See table on p.45.

Passive voice: The action of **a** VERB in the passive voice comes from the **AGENT**, which may or may not be included in the sentence. The SUBJECT is the PATIENT or the RECIPIENT: *The man* [subject, patient] *was arrested (by the police)* [agent] • *Fred* [subject, recipient] *was given a watch by his brother* [agent].

Patient: The object or person that is affected in some way by the action: *We ate the **cheese** • The curtain has been mended;* or effected: *We've made a **cake** • 'Skaters' was painted by Brueghel*.

Phrase: A group of words centred on a particular class of word (the HEAD): *lovely crunchy **biscuits*** (noun phrase) • *really **brilliant*** (adjective phrase) • ***on** the whole* (prepositional phrase). See tables on pp.57, 58, 60.

Phrasal verb: A verb consisting of 1) two parts: verb + PARTICLE: ***throw away**;* or verb + PREPOSITION: ***look through** the window*, or 2) three parts, verb + particle + preposition: ***put up with***. See tables on p.33, 34.

Possessive: A word denoting possession. PRONOUNS: ***mine, hers*** etc. DETERMINERS: ***my** books • **their** address* etc. Genitive form of the noun: ***John's** qualifications • **England's** rivers*.

Predicate: The part of the sentence that follows the SUBJECT: *Richard **eats prunes for breakfast***.

Preposition: A word occurring before a NOUN or NOUN PHRASE to indicate position: ***in** the field • **above** the table* or direction: ***towards** London • **into** the house* or, metaphorically, time: ***in** the morning • **at** Christmas* or in non-literal phrases: ***on** the whole • **with** respect*. See tables on pp.54, 55, 56.

Primary Auxiliary verb: 1) *be* and *have*. When placed before a main verb, these verbs have the function of determining ASPECT: *He **is** playing the piano • She **has** arrived* 2) *do* This verb is used in the interrogative and negative forms of the present and past simple tenses: ***Do** you like tea? • They **did**n't see the sign*. See tables on p.28.

Pronoun: A word used 1) to refer to things or persons whose identity is already established 2) to refer to something already mentioned in a text or discourse 3) to refer to something yet to be identified in a text or discourse 4) to call attention to something which is present to the senses 5) to introduce some types of relative clause. See table on p.14 for the different types.

Quantifier: An expression that indicates the set, or a subset, of a more or less well-defined entity or group. It occurs before a noun or noun phrase and includes the preposition *of*: *a **lot of** cheese • a **small number** of people*. See table on p.13.

Recipient: The receiver of a thing: *She gave **me** a new bicycle • I sent some flowers to **her***. In general, the recipient is represented by the indirect OBJECT.

Reciprocal verb: A verb which denotes reciprocal action: A does X to B and B does X to A: *They **kissed** (each other) • They didn't **recognise** one another*. Some reciprocal verbs must be followed by a reciprocal pronoun (*each other/one another*), while others don't require one.

Reflexive verb: A verb which is followed by a reflexive PRONOUN, indicating that the action is done by the subject to the subject: *He cut himself • They stuffed themselves*.

Relative clause: A clause typically beginning with a relative PRONOUN (*who, whom, which, that*) or relative adverb (*where, when*) which defines the SUBJECT or OBJECT of a verb (defining relative clause): *The man **who won the prize** lives in Manchester* or adds extra information about the subject or object (non-defining relative clause): *Jules Verne, **who wrote 20,000 Leagues under the Sea**, died in1905*. See table on p.64.

Simple sentence: A sentence which contains one SUBJECT and one VERB: *Geoffrey likes small dogs • They were driven to Portsmouth*. See tables on p.4 and p.74.

Stative verb: A verb which indicates a state rather than an action: *know, like, understand, contain, include*. See table on p.24.

Subject: The part of the sentence on which the rest depends, usually occurring before the verb: ***They*** *couldn't stand being told what to do* • ***The fridge*** *stands next to the cooker* • ***This bicycle*** *was made in Birmingham.*

Subordinate clause: A clause which is dependent on another clause, and which begins with a subordinating CONJUNCTION: *If they come…* • *Although he was tired …* • *Before it gets dark …* See table on p.62.

Subordination: The linking of a MAIN (independent) CLAUSE with a SUBORDINATE (dependent) clause: *When I smell tulips* [subordinate clause] *a shiver runs down my spine* [main clause].

Tense: A form of the verb indicating 1) present time: *She **runs** every day* 2) past time: *He **went** to the doctor's yesterday.* Each of these tenses combines with the progressive or perfective ASPECT, or both together. See tables on pp.41, 43.

Transitive verb: A verb which is followed by a direct object, indicating that the object is acted upon by the subject: *We* [subject] ***saw*** *the rainbow* [direct object] • *They **ate** all the rice.* See table on p.44.

Uncountable noun: A noun which cannot be preceded by a number or indefinite article and does not have a plural form: ***water, intelligence, sulphuric acid***. In practice, many nouns can be either countable or uncountable, depending on the context: *I want some coffee* [uncountable] • *three coffees* [countable]*, please.* See table on p.6.

Verb: A word which denotes a state, action or event. See STATIVE and DYNAMIC verbs.

Bibliography

Biber D., Johansson S., Leech G., Conrad S. and Finegan E. (1999)
Longman Grammar of Spoken and Written English (Pearson Education Ltd)

Carter R. and McCarthy M. (2006)
Cambridge Grammar of English: A Comprehensive Guide (CUP)

Chalker S. (1984) *Current English Grammar* (Macmillan)

Chalker S. and Weiner E. (1994) *The Oxford Dictionary of English Grammar* (OUP)

Cobbett W. (1832) *A Grammar of the English Language, in a Series of Letters* (New York)

Comrie B. (1985) *Tense* (Cambridge Textbooks in Linguistics) (CUP)

Crystal D. (1988) *Rediscover Grammar with David Crystal* (Longman)

Downing A. and Locke P. (1992) *A University Course in English Grammar* (Prentice Hall)

Huddleston R. and Pullum G.K. (2002) *The Cambridge Grammar of the English Language* (CUP)

Huddleston R. and Pullum G.K. (2005) *A Student's Introduction to English Grammar* (CUP)

Leech G. and Svartvik J. (1975) *A Communicative Grammar of English* (Longman)

Lock G. (1996) *Functional English Grammar* (CUP)

Parrott M. (2000) *Grammar for English Language Teachers* (CUP)

Quirk R., Greenbaum S., Leech G., and Svartvik J. (1985)
A Comprehensive Grammar of the English Language (Longman)

Sinclair J. et al (1990) *Collins COBUILD English Grammar* (HarperCollins)

Swan M. (2005) *Practical English Usage* (OUP)

Sweet H. (1903) *A New English Grammar: Logical and Historical, Part Two: Syntax* (Clarendon)

Thornbury S. (2005) *Uncovering Grammar* (Macmillan)

Woods E. (1995) *Introducing Grammar* (Penguin)